Continuous Testing

with Ruby, Rails, and JavaScript

Ben Rady
Rod Coffin

The Pragmatic Bookshelf

Dallas, Texas • Raleigh, North Carolina

Many of the designations used by manufacturers and sellers to distinguish their products are claimed as trademarks. Where those designations appear in this book, and The Pragmatic Programmers, LLC was aware of a trademark claim, the designations have been printed in initial capital letters or in all capitals. The Pragmatic Starter Kit, The Pragmatic Programmer, Pragmatic Programming, Pragmatic Bookshelf, PragProg and the linking *g* device are trademarks of The Pragmatic Programmers, LLC.

Every precaution was taken in the preparation of this book. However, the publisher assumes no responsibility for errors or omissions, or for damages that may result from the use of information (including program listings) contained herein.

Our Pragmatic courses, workshops, and other products can help you and your team create better software and have more fun. For more information, as well as the latest Pragmatic titles, please visit us at *http://pragprog.com*.

The team that produced this book includes:

Jacquelyn Carter (editor)
Potomac Indexing, LLC (indexer)
Kim Wimpsett (copyeditor)
David J Kelly (typesetter)
Janet Furlow (producer)
Juliet Benda (rights)
Ellie Callaghan (support)

Printed in the United States of America.
ISBN-13: 978-1-934356-70-8
Printed on acid-free paper.
Book version: P1.0—June 2011

Contents

Acknowledgments

We would like to thank everyone who offered encouragement and advice along the way, including our reviewers: Paul Holser, Noel Rappin, Bill Caputo, Fred Daoud, Craig Riecke, Slobodan (Dan) Djurdjevic, Ryan Davis, Tong Wang, and Jeff Sacks. Thanks to everyone at Improving Enterprises and the development team at Semantra for contributing to our research and helping us test our ideas. We'd like to thank Dave Thomas and Andy Hunt for giving us the opportunity to realize our vision for this book. Thanks also to our editor, Jackie Carter, for slogging alongside us week by week to help make that vision a reality.

We'd also like to thank all the Beta readers who offered feedback, including Alex Smith, Dennis Schoenmakers, "Johnneylee" Jack Rollins, Joe Fiorini, Katrina Owen, Masanori Kado, Michelle Pace, Olivier Amblet, Steve Nicholson, and Toby Joiner.

From Ben
I would like to thank my wife, Jenny, for supporting all of my crazy endeavors over the last few years, including this book. They've brought us joy and pain, but you've been by my side through it all. I'd also like to thank my mom, who first taught me the value of the written word and inspired me to use it to express myself.

From Rod
I would like to thank my wife for her encouragement and many sacrifices, my brother for his friendship, my mom for her unconditional love, and my dad for showing me how to be a husband, father, and citizen.

Preface

As professional programmers, few things instill more despair in us than discovering a horrible production bug in something that worked perfectly fine last week. The only thing worse is when our customers discover it and inform us...angrily. Automated testing, and particularly test driven development, were the first steps that we took to try to eliminate this problem. Over the last ten years, these practices have served us well and helped us in our fight against defects. They've also opened the doors to a number of other techniques, some of which may be even more valuable. Practices such as evolutionary design and refactoring have helped us deliver more valuable software faster and with higher quality.

Despite the improvements, automated testing was not (and is not) a silver bullet. In many ways, it didn't eliminate the problems we were trying to exterminate but simply moved them somewhere else. We found most of our errors occurring while running regression or acceptance tests in QA environments or during lengthy continuous integration builds. While these failures were better than finding production bugs, they were still frustrating because they meant we had wasted our time creating something that demonstrably did not work correctly.

We quickly realized that the problem in both cases was the timeliness of the feedback we were getting. Bugs that happen in production can occur weeks (or months or years!) after the bug is introduced, when the reason for the change is just a faint memory. The programmer who caused it may no longer even be on the project. Failing tests that ran on a build server or in a QA environment told us about our mistakes long after we'd lost the problem context and the ability to quickly fix them. Even the time between writing a test and running it as part of a local build was enough for us to lose context and make fixing bugs harder. Only by shrinking the gap between the creation of a bug and its resolution could we preserve this context and turn fixing a bug into something that is quick and easy.

While looking for ways to shrink those feedback gaps, we discovered continuous testing and started applying it in our work. The results were compelling. Continuous testing has helped us to eliminate defects sooner and given us the confidence to deliver software at a faster rate. We wrote this book to share these results with everyone else who has felt that pain. If you've ever felt fear in your heart while releasing new software into production, disappointment while reading the email that informs you of yet another failing acceptance test, or the joy that comes from writing software and having it work perfectly *the first time*, this book is for you.

Using continuous testing, we can immediately detect problems in code—before it's too late and before problems spread. It isn't magic but a clever combination of tests, tools, and techniques that tells us right away when there's a problem, not minutes, hours, or days from now but right now, when it's easiest to fix. This means we spend more of our time writing valuable software and less time slogging through code line by line and second-guessing our decisions.

Exploring the Chapters

This book is divided into two parts. The first part covers working in a pure Ruby environment, while the second discusses the application of continuous testing in a Rails environment. A good portion of the second part is devoted to continuous testing with JavaScript, a topic we believe deserves particular attention.

In Chapter 1, *Why Test Continuously?*, on page 1, we give you a bit of context. This chapter is particularly beneficial for those who don't have much experience writing automated tests. It also establishes some terminology we'll use throughout the book.

The next three chapters, Chapter 2, *Creating Your Environment*, on page 11, Chapter 3, *Extending Your Environment*, on page 37, and Chapter 4, *Interacting with Your Code*, on page 53, show how to create, enhance, and use a continuous testing environment for a typical Ruby project. We'll discuss the qualities of an effective suite of tests and show how continuous testing helps increase the quality of our tests. We'll take a close look at a continuous test runner, Autotest, and see how it can be extended to provide additional behavior that is specific to our project and its needs. Finally, we'll discuss some of the more advanced techniques that continuous testing allows, including inline assertions and comparison of parallel execution paths.

In the second part of the book, we create a CT environment for a Rails app. In addition to addressing some of the unique problems that Rails brings into the picture, we also take a look at another continuous test runner, Watchr. As we'll see, Watchr isn't so much a CT runner but a tool for easily creating feedback loops in our project. We'll use Watchr to create a CT environment for JavaScript, which will allow us to write tests for our Rails views that run very quickly and without a browser.

At the very end, we've also included a little "bonus" chapter: an appendix on using JavaScript like a functional programming language. If your use of JavaScript has been limited to simple HTML manipulations and you've never had the opportunity to use it for more substantial programming, you might find this chapter very enlightening.

For the most part, we suggest that you read this book sequentially. If you're very familiar with automated testing and TDD, you can probably skim through the first chapter, but most of the ideas in this book build on each other. In particular, even if you're familiar with Autotest, pay attention to the sections in Chapter 2, *Creating Your Environment*, on page 11 that discuss FIRE and the qualities of good test suites. These ideas will be essential as you read the later chapters.

Each chapter ends with a section entitled "Closing the Loop." In this section we offer a brief summary of the chapter and suggest some additional tasks or exercises you could undertake to increase your understanding of the topics presented in the chapter.

Terminology

We use the terms *test* and *spec* interchangeably throughout the book. In both cases, we're referring to a file that contains individual examples and assertions, regardless of the framework we happen to be working in.

We frequently use the term *production code* to refer to the code that is being tested by our specs. This is the code that will be running in production after we deploy. Some people call this the "code under test."

Who This Book Is For

Hopefully, testing your code continuously sounds like an attractive idea at this point. But you might be wondering if this book is really applicable to you and the kind of projects you work on. The good news is that the ideas we'll present are applicable across a wide range of languages, platforms, and projects. However, we do have a few expectations of you, dear reader. We're assuming the following things:

- You are comfortable reading and writing code.

- You have at least a cursory understanding of the benefits of automated testing.

- You can build tools for your own use.

Knowledge of Ruby, while very beneficial, isn't strictly required. If you're at all familiar with any object-oriented language, the Ruby examples will likely be readable enough that you will understand most of them. So if all of that sounds like you, we think you'll get quite a bit out of reading this book. We're hoping to challenge you, make you think, and question your habits.

Working the Examples

It's not strictly necessary to work through the examples in this book. Much of what we do with the examples is meant to spark ideas about what you should be doing in your own work rather than to provide written examples for you to copy. Nonetheless, working through some of the examples may increase your understanding, and if something we've done in the book would apply to a project that you're working on, certainly copying it verbatim may be the way to go.

To run the examples in this book, we suggest you use the following:

- A *nix operating system (Linux or MacOS, for example)

- Ruby 1.9.2

- Rails 3.0.4

In addition, you can find a list of the gems we used while running the examples in Appendix 2, *Gem Listing*, on page 133.

The examples may work in other environments (such as Windows) and with other versions of these tools, but this is the configuration that we used while writing the book.

Online Resources

The source for the examples is available at http://pragprog.com/titles/rcctr/source_code.

If you're having trouble installing Ruby, we suggest you try using the Ruby Version Manager (or RVM), available at: http://rvm.beginrescueend.com/.

If something isn't working or you have a question about the book, please let us know in the forums at http://forums.pragprog.com/forums/170.

Ben blogs at http://benrady.com, and you can find his Twitter stream at https://twitter.com/benrady.

Ben Rady
June 2011

Rod Coffin
June 2011

CHAPTER 1

Why Test Continuously?

Open your favorite editor or IDE. Take whatever key you have bound to Save and rebind it to Save and Run All Tests. Congratulations, you're now testing continuously.

If you create software for a living, the first thing that probably jumped into your head is, "That won't work." We'll address that issue later, but just for a moment, forget everything you know about software development as it is, pretend that it does work, and join us as we dream how things could be.

Imagine an expert, with knowledge of both the domain and the design of the system, pairing with you while you work. She tells you kindly, clearly, and concisely whenever you make a mistake. "I'm sorry," she says, "but you can't use a single string there. Our third-party payment system expects the credit card number as a comma-separated list of strings." She gives you this feedback constantly—every time you make any change to the code—reaffirming your successes and saving you from your mistakes.

Every project gets this kind of feedback *eventually*. Unfortunately for most projects, the time between when a mistake is made and when it is discovered is measured in days, weeks, or sometimes months. All too often, production problems lead to heated conversations that finally give developers the insights they wish they had weeks ago.

We believe in the value of *rapid* feedback loops. We take great care to discover, create, and maintain them on every project. Our goal is to reduce the length of that feedback loop to the point that it can be easily measured in milliseconds.

1.1 What Is Continuous Testing?

To accomplish this goal, we use a combination of tools and techniques we collectively refer to as *continuous testing*, or simply CT. A continuous testing environment validates decisions as soon as we make them. In this environment, every action has an opposite, automatic, and instantaneous reaction that tells us if what we just did was a bad idea. This means that making certain mistakes becomes impossible and making others is more difficult. The majority of the bugs that we introduce into our code have a very short lifespan. They never make their way into source control. They never break the build. They never sneak out into the production environment. Nobody ever sees them but us.

A CT environment is made up of a combination of many things, ranging from tools such as Autotest and Watchr to techniques such as behavior driven development. The tools constantly watch for changes to our code and run tests accordingly, and the techniques help us create informative tests. The exact composition of this environment will change depending on the language you're working in, the project you're working on, or the team you're working with. It cannot be created for you. You must build this environment as you build your system because it will be different for every project, every team, and every developer. The extent to which you're able to apply these principles will differ as well, but in all cases, the goal remains the same: instant and automatic validation of every decision we make.

1.2 Beyond Automated Tests

The primary tools we use to create environments for continuous testing are automated tests written by programmers as they write the production code. Many software development teams have recognized the design and quality benefits of creating automated test suites. As a result, the practice of automated testing—in one form or another—is becoming commonplace. In many cases, programmers are expected to be able to do it and do it well as part of their everyday work. Testing has moved from a separate activity performed by specialists to one that the entire team participates in. In our opinion, this is a very good thing.

Types of Tests

We strongly believe in automated testing and have used it with great success over many years. Over that time we've added a number of different types of automated tests to our arsenal. The first and most important of these is a *unit test*. The overwhelming majority (let's say 99.9%) of the tests we write are unit tests. These tests check very small bits of behavior, rarely larger than a single method or function. Often we'll have more than one individual test for a given method, even though the methods are not larger than half a dozen lines.

We don't like to run through complete use cases in a single unit test—invoking methods, making assertions, invoking more methods, and making more assertions. We find that tests that do that are generally brittle, and bugs in one part of the code can mask other bugs from being detected. This can result in us wasting time by introducing one bug while trying to fix another. We favor breaking these individual steps into individual tests. We'll take a closer look at the qualities of good tests in Section 2.2, *Creating a Potent Test Suite with FIRE*, on page 16.

Finding ourselves wanting to walk through a use case or other scenario in a unit test is a sign that we might need to create an acceptance test. Tools like Cucumber can be very useful for making these kinds of tests. While it's beyond the scope of this book, we would like to encourage you to check out Cucumber, and especially its use within the larger context of behavior driven development, at http://cukes.info/.

In addition to unit test and acceptance tests, we also employ other types of tests to ensure our systems work as expected. UI tests can check the behavior of GUI controls in various browsers and operating systems. Integration tests, for example, can be used when the components in our system wouldn't normally fail fast when wired together improperly. System tests can be used to verify that we can successfully deploy and start the system. Performance and load tests can tell us when we need to spend some time optimizing.

Using Automated Tests Wisely

As we mentioned earlier in the chapter, unit tests are our first and largest line of defense. We generally keep the number of higher level tests (system, integration, etc.) fairly small. We never verify business logic using higher level tests—that generally makes them too slow and brittle to be useful. This is especially true of UI tests, where testing business logic together with UI control behavior can lead to a maddening mess of interdependent failures. Decoupling the UI from the underlying system so the business logic can be mocked out for testing purposes is an essential part of this strategy.

The primary purpose of all of these tests is feedback, and the value of the tests is directly related to both the quality and timeliness of that feedback. We always run our unit tests continuously. Other types of tests are generally run on a need-to-know basis—that is, we run them when we need to know if they pass, but we can run any or all of these types of tests continuously if we design them to be run that way.

We don't have a lot of patience for tests that take too long to run, fail (or pass) unexpectedly, or generate obscure error messages when they fail. These tests are an investment, and like all investments, they must be chosen carefully. As we'll see, not only is continuous testing a way to get more out of the investment that we make in automated testing, but it's also a way to ensure the investments we make continue to provide good returns over time.

1.3 Enhancing Test Driven Development

If you're an experienced practitioner of test driven development, you may actually be very close to being able to test continuously. With TDD, we work by writing a very small test, followed by a minimal amount of production code. We then refactor to eliminate duplication and improve the design. With continuous testing, we get instant feedback at each of these steps, not just from the one test we happen to be writing but from all the relevant tests and with no extra effort or thinking on our part. This allows us to stay focused on the problem and the design of our code, rather than be distracted by having to run tests.

Both TDD and CT come from a desire for rapid feedback. In many ways, the qualities of a good continuous test suite are just the natural result of effectively applying test driven development. The difference is that while using continuous testing, you gain additional feedback loops. An old axiom of test driven development states that the tests test the correctness of the code, while the code, in turn, tests the correctness of the tests. The tests also test the design of the code—code that's poorly designed is usually hard to test. But what tests the design of the tests?

In our experience, continuous testing is an effective way to test the design and overall quality of our tests. As we'll see in Chapter 2, *Creating Your Environment*, on page 11, running our tests all the time creates a feedback loop that tells us when tests are misbehaving as we create them. This means we can correct existing problems faster and prevent bad tests from creeping into our system in the first place.

1.4 Continuous Testing and Continuous Integration

You might be familiar with the practice of continuous integration (CI) and wonder how it fits with continuous testing. We view them as complementary practices. Continuous testing is our first line of defense. Failure is extremely

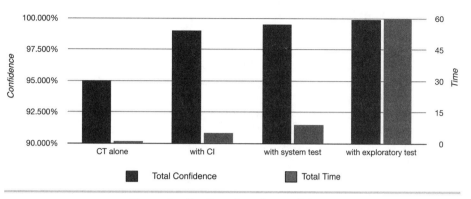

Figure 1—Trading time for confidence

cheap here, so this is where we want things to break most frequently. Running a full local build can take a minute or two, and we want our CT environment to give us the confidence we need to check in most of the time. Sometimes, we have particular doubts about a change we've made. Perhaps we've been mucking around in some configuration files or changing system seed data. In this case we might run a full build to be confident that things will work before we check in. Most of the time, however, we want to feel comfortable checking in whenever our tests pass in CT. If we don't have that confidence, it's time to write more tests.

Confidence, however, is not certainty. Continuous integration is there to catch problems, not just spend a lot of CPU time running tests that always pass. Sure, it helps us catch environmental problems, too (forgetting to check in a file, usually). But it can also serve as a way to offload the cost of running slower tests that rarely, but occasionally, fail. We don't check in code that we're not confident in, but at the same time, we're human and we sometimes make mistakes.

Every project and team can (and should) have a shared definition of what "confident" means. One way to think about it is as a series of feedback loops, all having an associated confidence and time cost. Take a look at Figure 1, *Trading time for confidence*, on page 5. This figure compares the confidence generated by the feedback loops in our project to their relative cost. As we move through our development process (left to right), total confidence in our code increases logarithmically, while the total cost to verify it increases exponentially.

You Broke the Build!

We've worked with a few teams that seemed to fear breaking the build. It's like they saw a continuous integration build as a test of programming prowess. Breaking it was a mortal sin, something to be avoided at all costs. Some teams even had little hazing rituals they would employ when the build broke, punishing the offender for carelessly defiling the code.

We think that attitude is a little silly. If the build never breaks, why even bother to have it? We think there is an optimal build success ratio for each project (ours usually runs around 90%+). We like being able to offload rarely failing tests to a CI server, and if that means we need to fix something one of every ten or twenty builds, so be it.

The important thing with broken builds is not that you try to avoid them at all costs but that you treat them seriously. Quite simply: stop what you're doing and fix it. Let everyone know that it's broken and that you're working on it. After all, nobody likes merging with broken code. But that doesn't mean breaking the build is "bad." Continuous integration is worth doing because it gives you feedback. If it never breaks, it's not telling you anything you didn't already know.

For example, in our continuous testing environment, we might spend a few seconds to be 95 percent sure that each change works properly. Once we have that confidence, we would be willing to let our CI server spend two minutes of its time running unit, integration, and system tests so that we're 95 percent confident we can deploy successfully. Once we deploy, we might do exploratory and acceptance testing to be 95 percent sure that our users will find sufficient value in this new version before we ship.

At each stage, we're trading some of our time in exchange for confidence that the system works as expected. The return we get on this time is proportional to how well we've maintained these feedback loops. Also note that the majority of our confidence comes from continuous testing, the earliest and fastest feedback loop in the process. If we have well-written, expressive tests that run automatically as we make changes, we can gain a lot of confidence very quickly. As a result, we spend a lot more of our time refining this environment because we get the greatest return on that time.

1.5 Learning to Test Continuously

If you think about it, continuous testing is just an extension of the Agile principles that we now take for granted. Many of the practices that developers employ today are designed to generate feedback. We demo our software to customers to get feedback on our progress. We hold retrospectives to get feedback about our process. Frequent releases allow us to get feedback from actual users about the value of our products. Test driven development was a revolution in software development that opened the doors to widespread use of rapid evolutionary design. By writing tests just before writing the code to make them pass, we act as consumers of our designs at the earliest possible moment—just before we create them.

One principle in particular, taken from Lean Software Development,[1] summarizes our thoughts on the value of feedback rather well. It states that in order to achieve high quality software, you have to *build quality in.* This does not mean "Try real hard not to make any mistakes." It's about actively building fail-safes and feedback mechanisms into every aspect of your project so that when things go wrong, you can recover quickly and gracefully. It's about treating these mechanisms with as much care as the product itself. It's about treating failure as an opportunity for learning and relentlessly searching for new opportunities to learn.

This book was written to teach you how to employ this valuable practice. In it, we'll show you how to create a customized environment for continuous testing using tools such as Autotest and Watchr. We'll cover the fundamentals of creating and maintaining a test suite that's fast, informative, reliable, and exhaustive.

Beyond just the basics of running tests, we'll introduce some advanced applications of continuous testing, such as inline assertions—a powerful alternative to debugging or console printing—and code path comparison. We'll show you how to apply these techniques and tools in other languages and frameworks, including Ruby on Rails and JavaScript. You'll be able to create feedback loops that validate decisions made outside of your code: you can automatically verify Rails migrations; instantly check changes to style sheets and views; and quickly validate documentation, seed data, and other essential configurations and settings.

We'll also see how continuous testing can help us improve the quality of existing tests and ensure that the new tests we write will do the job. By giving you instant feedback about the quality of your code and the quality of your tests, continuous testing creates a visceral feedback loop that you can actually feel as you work.

---

1. *Lean Software Development: An Agile Toolkit for Software Development Managers* [PP03]

Part I — Ruby and Autotest

CHAPTER 2

Creating Your Environment

If you're a typical Ruby developer, continuous testing is probably not a new idea to you. You may not have called it by that name, but chances are you can run your full build from Vim or TextMate with a single keystroke and you do this many, many times per day. This is a good thing.

Maintaining this rapid feedback loop as our projects grow larger and more complex requires that we take care in how we work. In this chapter, we'll discuss some well-known attributes of a healthy test suite and show why maintaining a healthy suite of tests is essential to creating a rapid, reliable test feedback loop. We'll see how continuous testing encourages writing good tests and how good tests benefit continuous testing.

2.1 Getting Started with Autotest

To get started, let's create a simple Ruby project. In this chapter, we're going to build a library that will help us analyze relationships on Twitter (a little social networking site you've probably never heard of). We're going to package our library as a Ruby gem, and to get started quickly, we're going to use a Ruby gem named Jeweler[1] to generate a project for us. Normally, we might use another tool, Bundler,[2] to create this gem, but for this example we use Jeweler for its scaffolding support. We can use it to generate a gem that includes a sample spec using RSpec, which helps us get started a little faster. Assuming you already have Ruby and RubyGems, installing is pretty easy.

```
$ gem install jeweler --version=1.5.2
$ jeweler --rspec twits
```

---

1. https://github.com/technicalpickles/jeweler

2. http://gembundler.com/

> ### Joe asks:
> ### What Is RSpec?
>
> In this book we use a framework called *RSpec* as our testing framework of choice because we like its emphasis on specifying behavior, given a context, rather than the flatter structure of Test::Unit. While the principles we discuss in this book can just as easily be applied when using another testing framework, we like using RSpec when working in Ruby because it helps communicate our intent very effectively.
>
> In RSpec, the files themselves are referred to as *specs*, while the individual test methods inside those specs are often called *examples*. Contexts, within which we can test the behavior of our classes and modules, can be specified by a describe() block. describe() blocks can also be nested, which gives us a lot of flexibility to describe the context in which behavior occurs.
>
> RSpec also integrates very nicely with Autotest and other continuous testing tools, so we'll be using it for the remainder of the book. We talk about the benefits of behavior driven development and RSpec in Section 2.3, *Writing Informative Tests*, on page 17, but to learn more about RSpec in depth, visit http://rspec.info or get *The RSpec Book* [CADH09] by David Chelimsky and others.

This command tells Jeweler to create a Ruby gem project in a directory named twits.[3] Because we installed the gem for RSpec and used the --rspec option, Jeweler set up this project to be tested with RSpec. It created a dummy spec in the spec directory named twits_spec.rb. It also created a file in that directory named spec_helper.rb, which our specs will use to share configuration code.

So Jeweler has generated a project for us with some specs, but how are we going to run them? Well, we could run them with the command rake spec, and, just to make sure things are working properly, we'll go ahead and do that. First we need to finish setting up our project by having Bundler install any remaining gems. Then we can run our tests.

```
$ cd twits
$ bundle install
$ rake

F

Failures:

  1) Twits fails
```

---

3. If you're having trouble getting this command to run, you may need to install Git, which is available at http://git-scm.com/.

```
      Failure/Error: specing for real"
      RuntimeError:
        Hey buddy, you should rename this file and start specing for real
      # ./code/ruby/twits/spec/revisions/twits2.1_spec_fail.rb:6:in
`block (2 levels) in <top (required)>'

Finished in 0.00031 seconds
1 example, 1 failure
```

Great. However, seeing as how this is a book on running tests continuously, we should probably find a faster way than running rake commands. One such way is to use Autotest, a continuous test runner for Ruby. Whenever you change a file, Autotest runs the corresponding tests for you. It intelligently selects the tests to be run based on the changes we make. Autotest is going to be running our tests for us as we work on our gem, so we can focus on adding value (rather than on running tests). Installing Autotest is pretty easy. It's included in the ZenTest gem:

```
$ gem install ZenTest --version=4.4.2
```

Now that we have Autotest installed, let's start it from the root of our project:

```
$ autotest

F

Failures:

  1) Twits fails
     Failure/Error: specing for real"
     RuntimeError:
       Hey buddy, you should rename this file and start specing for real
     # ./code/ruby/twits/spec/revisions/twits2.1_spec_fail.rb:6:in
`block (2 levels) in <top (required)>'

Finished in 0.00031 seconds
1 example, 1 failure
```

Yay, it fails! Autotest now detected our Jeweler-generated spec and ran it. Now let's go make it pass. Open up your favorite editor and take a look at spec/twits_spec.rb. You should see something like this:

```
ruby/twits/spec/revisions/twits2.1_spec_fail.rb
require File.expand_path(File.dirname(__FILE__) + '/../spec_helper')

describe "Twits" do
  it "fails" do
    fail "Hey buddy, you should rename this file and start specing for real"
  end
end
```

> ## Behind the Magic
>
> Autotest doesn't really know anything about RSpec, so the fact that this just seemed to work out of the box is a bit surprising. There's actually some rather sophisticated plugin autoloading going on behind the scenes (that we'll discuss in depth in a later chapter). For now, just be thankful the magic is there.
>
> If, however, you have other projects that use RSpec and you want to use Autotest like this, you're going to want to make sure that there's a .rspec file in the root of your project. This file can be used to change various settings in RSpec (--color, for example). More importantly for us, its presence tells Autotest to run RSpec specs instead of tests.

Then we remove the call to fail:

```
ruby/twits/spec/revisions/twits2.1_spec.rb
require File.expand_path(File.dirname(__FILE__) + '/../spec_helper')

describe "Twits" do
  it "fails" do
  end
end
```

When we save our change, Autotest should detect that a file has changed and rerun the appropriate test:

```
.


Finished in 0.00027 seconds
1 example, 0 failures
```

Success!

Notice that we didn't have to tell Autotest to run. It detected the change to twits_spec.rb and ran the test automatically. From now on, any change we make to a file will trigger a test run. This isn't limited to test files either. Any change that we make to any Ruby file in our project will trigger a test run. Because of this, we'll never have to worry about running tests while we work.

Autotest runs different sets of tests, depending on which tests fail and what you change. By only running certain tests, we can work quickly while still getting the feedback we want. We refer to this approach of running a subset of tests as *test selection*, and it can make continuous testing viable on much larger and better tested projects.

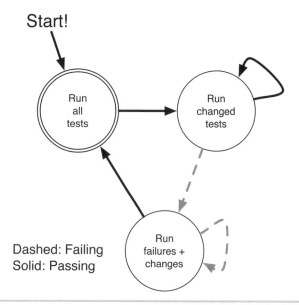

Start!

Run all tests

Run changed tests

Run failures + changes

Dashed: Failing
Solid: Passing

Figure 2—The Autotest lifecycle

As we can see in Figure 2, *The Autotest lifecycle*, on page 15, Autotest selects tests thusly: When it starts, Autotest runs all the tests it finds. If it finds failing tests, it keeps track of them. When changes are made, it runs the corresponding tests plus any previously failing tests. It continues to do that on each change until no more tests fail. Then it runs all the tests to make sure we didn't break anything while it was focused on errors and changes.

Like a spellchecker that highlights spelling errors as you type or a syntax checker in an IDE, continuous testing provides instant feedback about changes as you make them. By automatically selecting and running tests for us, Autotest allows us to maintain focus on the problem we're trying to solve, rather than switching contexts back and forth between working and poking the test runner. This lets us freely make changes to the code with speed and confidence. It transforms testing from an *action* that must be thoughtfully and consciously repeated hundreds of times per day into what it truly is: a *state*. So rather than thinking about when and how to run our tests, at any given moment we simply know that they are either passing or failing and can act accordingly.

2.2 Creating a Potent Test Suite with FIRE

Of course, Autotest isn't going to do all the work for us. We still need to create a suite of tests for it to run. Not only that, if we want Autotest to continue to give us this instant feedback as our projects grow larger, there are some guidelines we're going to have to follow. Otherwise, the rapid feedback loop Autotest creates for us will slowly grind to a halt.

In order to get the most valuable feedback possible from a continuous test runner like Autotest, the tests in our suite need to be *fast*, so that we can run them after every change. They need to be *informative*, so we know what's broken as soon as it breaks. They need to be *reliable*, so we can be highly confident in the results. Finally, they need to be *exhaustive*, so that every change we make is validated. When our test suite has all of these attributes (summarized in the handy acronym *FIRE*), it becomes easy to run those tests continuously.

*F*ast

*I*nformative

*R*eliable

*E*xhaustive

Continuous testing creates multiple feedback loops. While CT will tell us whether our tests pass or fail, it also tells us a lot more by running them all the time. By shifting the focus from merely automatic feedback to instant feedback,[4] we gain insight into how well we're writing our tests. CT exposes the weak points in our code and gives us the opportunity to fix problems as soon as they arise. In this way, continuous testing turns the long-term concerns of maintaining a test suite into immediate concerns.

Without this additional feedback loop, it's easy to get complacent about maintaining our tests. Automated testing is often an investment in future productivity. It's sometimes tempting to take shortcuts with tests in order to meet short-term goals. Continuous testing helps us stay disciplined by providing both positive and negative reinforcement. A FIREy test suite will

---

4. For sufficiently large values of "instant"—not more than a few seconds

Joe asks:

Is Autotest Really Going to Run ALL of My Tests on Every Change?

No. Autotest uses some heuristics to pick which tests to run. If you're starting Autotest for the first time, it does indeed run all the tests to see which ones (if any) are failing. After that, it will only run all the tests if there are no failures. As soon as Autotest detects a failure, it will only run the failing tests and the tests that are *mapped* with the files you change.

So what does "mapped" mean? It depends on what kind of project you're in. For example, if you're using Test::Unit in a regular Ruby project, Autotest maps tests in the test/ directory, refixed with test_, to similarly named files in the lib/ directory. So if you change a file named foo.rb, Autotest will run test_foo.rb.

You can configure these mappings yourself, if you like, and various Autotest plugins can create mappings for you. We'll take a closer look at configuring Autotest mapping and Autotest plugins in *Mapping Tests to Resources*, on page 42.

provide us with the immediate pass/fail feedback we want. As we'll see later, it also forms an effective foundation for other types of valuable feedback loops. On the other hand, if we start to stray off the path of good testing, CT lets us know we've strayed by exposing our pain sooner. In short, *if it hurts, you're doing it wrong.*

However, if we're going to use pain as a feedback mechanism, we need to know how to interpret the pain we're feeling. Merely knowing that something is wrong doesn't tell us how to fix it. It's essential that you clearly understand why each of the FIRE attributes is important, what will happen if your test suite is lacking in one (or more) of them, and what you can do to prevent those kinds of problems.

There's a big difference between knowing all the possible "good" things you could do and doing the specific things you need to do to achieve a particular goal. In this section, we're going to look at some specific attributes of our tests that can be improved with continuous testing. As we examine these four attributes in depth, think about problems you've had with tests in the past and whether testing continuously would have helped expose the causes of those problems. We're going to start with the *I* in FIRE: *informative.*

2.3 Writing Informative Tests

It's easy to focus on classes and methods when writing tests. Many developers believe that you should pair each production class with a test case and each method on that class with its own test method. There's a lot of material out there on automated testing that suggests that you should write tests this way. It may be expedient and familiar, but is it really the best way?

Our goal in writing informative tests is to communicate with the other developers who will be maintaining our code. More often than not, those other developers are us just weeks or months from now, when the context of what we were doing has been lost. Tests that merely repeat the structure of the code don't really help us that much when we're trying to understand why things are the way they are. They don't provide any new information, and so when they fail, all we know is that something is wrong.

Imagine that six months from now, we're happily coding along when a test suddenly fails. What do we want it to tell us? If all it says is that the call to create_registration_token() returned nil when it expected 7, we'll be left asking the question *why?* Why is it now nil? Is nil a valid state for a token? What does 7 mean anyway? What do we use these registration tokens for and when would we create one? Continuously running confusing tests like this can be more distracting than helpful. If each change you make assaults you with failures that each take minutes to diagnose, you'll quickly feel the pain of uninformative tests.

Behavior Driven Development

Behavior driven development (BDD) grew out of a desire to improve the practice of test driven development. From themes to stories to acceptance tests, BDD in the scope of project management is a much larger topic than would be appropriate to cover here. But within the scope of writing informative tests, it makes sense for us to focus on a particular aspect of BDD: writing specs (or unit tests, as they're sometimes called).

As the name implies, behavior driven development emphasizes behavior over structure. Instead of focusing on classes and methods when writing our tests, we focus on the valuable behavior our system should exhibit. As we build the classes that make up our Ruby application, this focus on behavior will ensure that the tests we write inform future maintainers of our software of its purpose, down to the lowest levels of the code. As a result, BDD style tests often read like sentences in a specification.

Behavior and Context

So we've started working on twits, and Autotest has helped us quickly identify when our changes cause tests to pass or fail. Now we need to add a little bit of functionality—something that will allow us to get the last five tweets

> ## Don't Duplicate Your Design
>
> Naming our tests based on the structure of our code has a painful side effect: it creates duplication. If we write test methods like test_last_five_tweets() and we rename the last_five_tweets() method, we'll have to remember to update the test as well (or, more than likely, we'll forget to update it and wind up with a very confusing and uninformative test). For all the reasons why duplication is evil, naming your tests this way is a bad idea.
>
> By definition, refactoring is improving the design and structure of code without changing its behavior. By naming our tests after the behavior we want rather than the structure of the code, not only do we make them more informative but we also make refactoring less costly.

that a user has tweeted. As we saw in Section 2.1, *Getting Started with Autotest*, on page 11, we're using RSpec to test our code in twits, so step one in creating this new functionality is to make a new spec.

Our first opportunity to create an informative test comes when choosing the outer structure of the test. Usually, the outer describe() block in a spec specifically names the class or module that provides the behavior we want to test. But it's important to note that it could just as easily be a string that describes where that behavior comes from.

ruby/twits/spec/revisions/user2.1_spec.rb
```
require File.expand_path(File.dirname(__FILE__) + '/../spec_helper')

describe "Twitter User" do
end
```

In this case, "Twitter User" seems more appropriate than merely the class name, User. As we discussed earlier in this chapter, we don't want to rely simply on the structure of our code to guide the structure of our tests. The emphasis is always on behavior in a given context.

Let's describe that context a little more clearly with another describe() block:

ruby/twits/spec/revisions/user2.2_spec.rb
```
describe "Twitter User" do
  describe "with a username" do
  end
end
```

So here we're specifying that a user has an associated Twitter username. Note that we haven't yet defined how the User class is related to that username. At this point, we don't care. We're just trying to capture a description of our context.

Now that we have that context, we can start to get a little more specific about what it means using a before() block in our spec:

```
ruby/twits/spec/revisions/user2.3_spec.rb
describe "Twitter User" do
  describe "with a username" do
    before( :each ) do
      @user = User.new
      @user.twitter_username = 'logosity'
    end
  end
end
```

The before() block here acts as the concrete definition of what this context means. It means that we have a User instance with the twitter_username set to the string value 'logosity'. This instance is available to all the examples in this context via the @user variable. Of course, the User class doesn't exist yet, so the failure of this test will drive us to create it:

```
ruby/twits/lib/revisions/user2.1.rb
class User
  attr_accessor :twitter_username
end
```

Now that we've described the context that we're working in, it's time to focus on behavior. We need the user to provide the last five tweets from Twitter, so we're going to write an example that captures that:

```
ruby/twits/spec/revisions/user2.4_spec.rb
describe "Twitter User" do
  describe "with a username" do
    before( :each ) do
      @user = User.new
      @user.twitter_username = 'logosity'
    end

    it "provides the last five tweets from Twitter" do
    end

  end
end
```

That looks about right.

Again, note that we're focused on describing the behavior first, before we write any code or even any assertions. Now that we've described what we want, we can get specific about how to get it (and how to test for it).

```
ruby/twits/spec/revisions/user2.5_spec.rb
describe "Twitter User" do
  describe "with a username" do
    before( :each ) do
      @user = User.new
      @user.twitter_username = 'logosity'
    end

    it "provides the last five tweets from Twitter" do
      @user.last_five_tweets.should have(5).tweets
    end
  end
end
```

Be aware that the have matcher in RSpec accepts almost any method invocation and simply ignores it. The call to tweets() in this case is purely to make the assertion more expressive.

As soon as we add this assertion, Autotest begins to fail:

```
F

Failures:

  1) Twitter User with a username provides the last five tweets from twitter
     Failure/Error: @user.last_five_tweets.should have(5).tweets
     NoMethodError: undefined method `last_five_tweets' for
#<User:0x000001010f8028 @twitter_username="logosity">
     # ./code/ruby/twits/spec/revisions/user2.4_spec_fail.rb:13:in
`block (3 levels) in <top (required)>'

Finished in 0.00057 seconds
1 example, 1 failure
```

At this point—and no sooner—we want to focus on how exactly we are going to get this information from Twitter. For now, we're going to "fake it until we make it" by returning an array of five elements:

```
ruby/twits/lib/revisions/user2.5.rb
class User
  attr_accessor :twitter_username

  def last_five_tweets
    return [1, 2, 3, 4, 5]
  end
end
```

After all, that's the only behavior that this test (in its current state) is specifying. If we added any more, it would be untested.

By writing our specs this way, we ensure that a failure reveals its intent. We know why this spec was written. We know what behavior it expects. If we can't quickly answer these questions after reading a failing test, we'll be in a world of hurt. We'll know that something is broken, but we won't know what. This can be incredibly frustrating and, without informative tests, much too common. BDD encourages us to write tests that explain themselves. So if we were to make this spec fail by removing one of the elements in our array of "tweets," we'd immediately get a failure in Autotest that looked like this:

```
F

Failures:

  1) Twitter User with a username provides the last five tweets from
twitter
     Failure/Error: @user.last_five_tweets.should have(5).tweets
       expected 5 tweets, got 4
     # ./code/ruby/twits/spec/revisions/user2.5_spec_fail.rb:13:in
`block (3 levels) in <top (required)>'

Finished in 0.00049 seconds
1 example, 1 failure
```

Notice how in this failure message RSpec combined the contents of our describe clauses with the name of the example to describe the failure in this way:

```
'Twitter User with a username provides the last five tweets from Twitter'
```

Explaining the behavior in this way also gives us feedback about the behavior that we're defining. What if the user doesn't have a Twitter account name in the system? Should we return nil? An empty array? Raise an exception? Just as explaining your problem to someone else can trigger an insight (regardless of whether or not they were actually listening to you), being very specific about exactly what you're testing can help you spot gaps and clarify what really needs to be done. In our case, once this example passes, perhaps we need to add another one, like this:

```
it "should not provide tweets if it does not have a Twitter username"
```

Regardless of whether you use RSpec, it's essential that your tests communicate context and behavior rather than setup and structure. In many cases, this is as much about what you don't assert as what you do. For example, notice that nothing in this spec tests that the Twitter API works. When choosing what to assert, put yourself in the shoes of a developer who has just changed your implementation and is now staring at your failing example. Would this assertion explain to them why that behavior was needed, or is it just checking an implementation detail that doesn't really affect the behavior? If you're not sure, try making an inconsequential change to your code and see if something breaks.

2.4 Writing Fast Tests

Even if you're not running them continuously, a good unit test suite should be fast. If you're going to run your tests continuously, however, they have to be fast. If our tests aren't fast enough, we're going to feel it, and it's going to hurt.

So how fast are "fast" tests? Fast enough to run hundreds of tests per second. A little math will tell you that a single "fast" test method will run in less than ten milliseconds. Submillisecond runtime is a good goal to aim for. This means you should be able to add thousands of tests to your system without taking any special measures to speed them up. We want our primary CT feedback loop to run in a second or two (including process startup time), and we generally think of one minute as the maximum tolerable amount of time for a full integration build. Past that, and we start looking for ways to make things faster.

The good news is that the vast majority of the time, test slowness is caused by one thing: leaving the process. Any I/O outside the current process, such as database or filesystem calls, pretty much guarantees that your test will run in more than ten milliseconds. More flagrant violations like remote network access can result in tests that take hundreds of milliseconds to run. So if we want to fight slow tests, the first attack is on I/O in all its forms. Thankfully, Ruby gives us a wide array of tools to handle this problem.

Introducing IO

In the previous section, we created a test for last_five_tweets(), but our implementation is a little lacking. Now we need to focus on driving that fakery out of our User class with a test that forces us to interact with the Twitter API. Just to get started, we'll encode logosity's last five tweets in a spec:

```
ruby/twits/spec/revisions/user2.6_spec_fail.rb
describe "Twitter User" do
  describe "with a username" do
    before( :each ) do
      @user = User.new
      @user.twitter_username = 'logosity'
    end
```

```
    it "provides the last five tweets from Twitter" do
      tweets = [
        "The only software alliance that matters is the one you forge
          with your coworkers",
        "The only universal hedge is firepower
          #zombieoranyotherapocolypse",
        "Thursday is Friday's Friday",
        "Never let the facts get in the way of a good argument",
        "Henceforth always refer to scrum in the past tense"
      ]

      @user.last_five_tweets.should == tweets
    end
  end
end
```

Saving that gives us a failing test in Autotest:

```
F

Failures:

  1) Twitter User with a username provides the last five tweets from
twitter
     Failure/Error: @user.last_five_tweets.should == tweets
       expected: ["The only software alliance that matters is the one
you forge\n          with your coworkers", "The only universal hedge
is firepower \n          #zombieoranyotherapocolypse", "Thursday is
Friday's Friday", "Never let the facts get in the way of a good
argument", "Henceforth always refer to scrum in the past tense"]
            got: [1, 2, 3, 4, 5] (using ==)
       Diff:
       @@ -1,6 +1,2 @@
       -["The only software alliance that matters is the one you
forge\n          with your coworkers",
       - "The only universal hedge is firepower \n
#zombieoranyotherapocolypse",
       - "Thursday is Friday's Friday",
       - "Never let the facts get in the way of a good argument",
       - "Henceforth always refer to scrum in the past tense"]
       +[1, 2, 3, 4, 5]
     # ./code/ruby/twits/spec/revisions/user2.6_spec_fail.rb:23:in
`block (3 levels) in <top (required)>'

Finished in 0.00157 seconds
1 example, 1 failure
```

Now we go and add the Twitter gem to our Gemfile (there's a gem for Twitter, right? Yep, of course there is). Why not just install it using the gem command?

Well, unlike the other gems we've installed, this one is actually going to be required by the twits gem itself, so we need to make sure it's included in the Gemfile. That way it will be installed automatically when other people use our gem:

ruby/twits/Gemfile
```
gem 'twitter', '1.1.1'
```

And after reading the documentation a little bit, we can go ahead and make a call to the service using the user's Twitter ID:

ruby/twits/lib/revisions/user2.7.rb
```
require 'twitter'

class User
  attr_accessor :twitter_username

  def last_five_tweets
    return Twitter::Search.new.per_page(5).from(@twitter_username).map do |tweet|
      tweet[:text]
    end.to_a
  end
end
```

A quick save...

```
Finished in 0.854569 seconds.
2 tests, 1 assertion, 0 failures, 0 errors
```

and our test passes.

Breaking Dependencies

So that passes, but as it stands there are a number of problems with this test. What happens if Twitter goes down? What if we want to work offline? The expectations in this test are based on the current state of the world; what if @logosity tweets something else?

The first problem we're going to want to correct, however, is the slowness of the test. Notice the timing information that Autotest reports for this one test. It takes almost a full second to run! Anything that affects the speed of our feedback loop must be addressed immediately. If we don't fix this now, we'll be paying the cost of that slow test every time we make a change to correct any other problem. Thankfully, we can use a mocking framework to break the dependency on the Twitter web API call to speed up the test and make it more consistent. RSpec comes with its own mocking framework, so we're going to use that to improve our test:

```
ruby/twits/spec/revisions/user2.7_spec.rb
it "provides the last five tweets from Twitter" do
  tweets = [
    {:text => 'tweet1'},
    {:text => 'tweet2'},
    {:text => 'tweet3'},
    {:text => 'tweet4'},
    {:text => 'tweet5'}
  ]

  mock_client = mock('client')
  mock_client.should_receive(:per_page).with(5).and_return(mock_client)
  mock_client.should_receive(:from).with('logosity').and_return(tweets)
  Twitter::Search.should_receive(:new).and_return(mock_client)

  @user.last_five_tweets.should == %w{tweet1 tweet2 tweet3 tweet4 tweet5}
end
```

In this test, mock_client acts as a fake for the real Twitter client. Twitter has a fluent API, so the calls to set search options like max() return a reference to the Twitter client itself. That's why the expectation for the call to per_page() returns mock_client, while the expectation for from() returns the actual tweets. Finally, we replace the default implementation of new() on Twitter::Search with one that returns our mock client, so that when we invoke last_five_tweets(), the mock is used.

```
Finished in 0.044423 seconds.

2 tests, 5 assertions, 0 failures, 0 errors
```

Notice how much faster the new version of this test runs. And some of the other problems we were seeing earlier have also vanished. A user account could be deleted and the test would still pass. Twitter can go down and it will still pass. The entire Internet could be destroyed in a tragic blimp accident, and we would still be verifying that last_five_tweets() works. Slowness is an excellent indicator of other problems with a test, which is yet another reason why we make it pass, then make it fast.

Even if we're writing our tests first, we still need to be aware of the design decisions that the tests are driving us toward. Just calling out to this external service might seem like the simplest thing that could possibly work. Indeed, using that approach first ensured that we understood exactly how the real Twitter client behaves and that we expected the right kind of data. But it's essential that we not leave the test in this state. Maintaining a fast test suite requires that we provide mechanisms for decoupling external dependencies from the rest of our code. This not only makes continuous testing possible but also helps improve our design.

Beware of Timers

One common barrier to creating a fast test suite is that the difference between 1 ms and 150 ms isn't really noticeable when you're running only one test. Unless you pay very close attention to the timing information reported by your CT runner, you may not notice that the test you're writing has become slow. When you have thousands of tests in your suite, however, it's *very* noticeable. Unfortunately, at that point it's also very expensive to fix.

So we might be inclined to add in special checks to ensure our tests run quickly. Add a cutoff—let's say, 50 ms—and fail any test that runs slower than that. Seems reasonable, right? Unfortunately, we haven't had much luck using this approach to detect slow tests. We always seem to wind up with a lot of false positives, which are quite distracting.

The problem is that on any given programmer's workstation, there are probably a few dozen different processes running, vying for the shared resources of the machine. If one of them suddenly needs a lot of time on the CPU in the middle of your test run, you might wind up with a few tests that take ten times longer (or more) than usual. That's why we think of fast tests as meaning that potentially hundreds of tests can be run per second rather than 1 ms or 5 ms per test. While the time-per-test average for a whole suite of tests might be between 1 and 5 ms, the time it takes to run one individual test can vary greatly depending on exactly what was going on with your computer when that test was run.

The one way we have found to get a reliable measure of how long a test takes is to run it enough times to even out any inconsistencies in the runtime environment. This usually means running it many thousands of times. While this might be acceptable for a performance test, taking this much time to run a unit test—just so you can measure how slow it is—is rather silly.

So rather than use timers to try to detect slow tests, we tend to stay on the lookout for the root causes of slowness. By writing focused and decoupled unit tests that stay away from the filesystem, the network, and other expensive shared resources, we can ensure our tests run quickly without having to measure how quickly each individual test runs.

2.5 Writing Reliable Tests

Put simply, a reliable test is one that only fails when something is broken and only passes when something works. If all of our tests pass, we should have confidence that all the valuable behaviors we expect to have in our system are present. If one of our tests fails, we should have confidence that whatever we just did has changed behavior in the system that we previously thought was valuable. While it seems obvious that our tests should be reliable, there are many subtle ways that they can become unreliable.

Assert Something

We sometimes find that developers write tests with no assertions. They set up a class, call a method, and then do nothing with the result. While it is certainly possible to reproduce some kinds of bugs this way, it doesn't really ensure the test will fail when something is broken. We think that writing a test without an assertion is like trying to teach a pig to sing: it wastes your time and annoys the pig. For instance, without looking at the implementation, can you tell what this zip_code() example is supposed to verify?

```
ruby/twits/spec/revisions/user2.8_spec.rb
it "should allow addresses with no zip code" do
  user = User.new
  user.address_text = 'P.O. BOX 7122 Chicago, IL'
  user.zip_code
end
```

While this does verify that zip_code() will not raise an error if you don't have a zip in the address, is that really sufficient? It doesn't really tell us what the User class should *do*. Should it return nil? A blank String?

Let's say the zip_code() method is implemented as follows:

```
ruby/twits/lib/revisions/user2.8.rb
def zip_code
  m = /\d\d\d\d\d/.match(address_text)
  return m[0] if m
end
```

As it turns out, this implementation returns nil if the address does not have a zip code. As we build other parts of our system, we might come to depend on that behavior. For example, blank strings are *truthy* (they evaluate to true as booleans), while nil is *falsey*. If we have any code that checks for a zip code like this:

```
ruby/twits/lib/revisions/user2.8.rb
def nearby_followers(user)
  return [] unless user.zip_code
  # Find followers of the given user in the same and surrounding zip code
  # ...
end
```

No Assertions Throw Off Coverage Reports

Tests with no assertions create another problem: they throw off code coverage metrics. While code coverage isn't a perfect measure of how well tested your system is, it can tell you what areas are totally untested. If we have untested areas of code in our system, we want our coverage report to show that so we can take appropriate steps to add tests when necessary. If our code is covered but not tested by examples with no assertions, then those problems are masked. We're left to find those untested areas the hard way.

and we later change the implementation of zip_code() to return a blank string, that check for the zip code will always pass, creating problems further down the line. Our original test for missing zip codes might run immediately, but it won't fail. There will be nothing to tell us that we've broken something. No matter how often you run them, tests that don't fail when things are broken just aren't that valuable.

So let's try to add an assertion to this test. Let's assume that we decide that the best course of action is to return nil. Now that we've decided what the behavior should be, we can not only add an assertion but improve the name of the example as well:

```
ruby/twits/spec/revisions/user2.8_spec.rb
it "should treat missing zip codes as nil" do
  user = User.new
  user.address_text = 'P.O. BOX 7122 Chicago, IL'
  user.zip_code.should be nil
end
```

So if we come along later and change the implementation to return a blank string instead, we immediately get this from Autotest:

```
'Twitter User should treat missing zip codes as nil' FAILED
expected nil, got ""
```

It's plain as day what we did, why it was wrong, and how to fix it.

Stay off the Network

As we saw in Section 2.4, *Writing Fast Tests*, on page 23, connecting to a public website like Twitter can not only cause our tests to run slowly but also make them unreliable. While this may seem obvious (especially given the "fail whale" frequency of Twitter), connecting to seemingly more stable network resources can also create unreliable tests. Not only can calls to databases, domain controllers, directory services, email servers, and other local network resources cause your tests to run slower, but they may cause your tests to fail at unexpected or inopportune times.

Imagine a scenario where some critical network service, like an authentication controller, goes down. You're called upon to create an emergency patch to work around the problem. If some or all of your tests depend on that controller, you'll be stuck in a catch-22, unable to fix a problem because the problem is getting in your way. You'll have to disable all of your tests to make progress. Then you'll be under pressure to get something fixed without the safety net of continuous testing to ensure you're not breaking something else in the process—a dangerous combination, to be sure.

Watch Out for Threads

If you're working in a multithreaded system, you may have state that is shared between the threads. If you don't, count yourself lucky. If you do, you'll have to take steps to ensure that you're synchronizing the threads properly when accessing that data. Of course, if we want to be sure that synchronization works properly, we're going to have to test it. This is a difficult problem and one of the more daunting challenges for the test driven developer. Writing a multithreaded system is hard. Writing one that can be tested to ensure it works 100 percent of the time is even harder. Fortunately, continuous testing can offer us some help.

Many threading problems manifest themselves as very rare timing errors (that only seem to occur in production). The failures may only occur one out of every thousand or ten thousand executions, usually without explanation or apparent cause. Often, these problems are caused by *race conditions*, where the specific timing of two or more interacting threads causes an error to occur. Few things in software development are more frustrating than a race condition that only shows up sometimes.

However, as a natural side effect of running an optimized set of tests, our tests are run in many different orders and combinations. In our experience, this constant reshuffling of tests is often able to identify synchronization problems in multithreaded code. The secret is to pay attention. These kinds of problems are, by their very nature, transient. If you get an unexpected failure in a multithreaded class after making a seemingly unrelated change, you may have just discovered a race condition. Make the same change again and see if the test starts to pass all of the sudden. If it does pass, you do indeed have a problem.

> ## Threading in Ruby
>
> Most Ruby VMs, like the reference implementation YARV, have a global interpreter lock, or GIL, that prevents more than one thread from executing at a time. As a result, threads in Ruby are somewhat less useful than they are in other languages that are fully multithreaded.
>
> However, just because only one thread can be running at a time doesn't mean you can ignore the problems of thread synchronization. Any data that is modified in a less-than-atomic operation is suspect. That operation could be preempted midway, meaning that another thread accessing that data would get an incomplete or inaccurate result.

Or, more accurately, what you have is a gift from the programming gods. Knowing that you have a synchronization problem is the first step in correcting it, and knowing about it while you're still working on the system is orders of magnitude better than having to diagnose what's going on after you've released. Better still, knowing the specific test that manifested the problem can give you great insight into what's going on. As strange as it is to say, these kinds of random test failures can be your friend. They're often a clue to more serious problems that would otherwise go undetected.

Temporal Dependencies

Global variables are—for lack of a better word—evil. In object-oriented languages, we sometimes find global variables masquerading as something seemingly more innocuous (like a class variable), but the evil is still there. If this state is not carefully (or better yet, automatically) cleaned up after each test, a *temporal dependency* can be created. This may cause tests to pass or fail, depending on which order they are run in. As you can imagine, avoiding this situation is essential to creating a reliable test suite.

Let's say that we have a request for that universal software monkey wrench, internationalization! Now we've got to handle all sorts of formats for addresses, depending on our locale. To facilitate this, we're going to create a Locale class that holds the current locale, which we can then use to parse location sensitive data (like our zip code). As always, we start with a test:

ruby/twits/spec/revisions/user2.9_spec.rb
```ruby
it "uses the current locale to parse zip codes" do
  Locales.current = Locales::UNITED_KINGDOM
  user = User.new
  user.address_text = '51-55 Gresham Street, 6th Floor London, England EC2V 7HQ'
  user.zip_code.should == 'EC2V 7HQ'
end
```

This drives out the corresponding changes to User and the new Locales module:

ruby/twits/lib/revisions/user2.9.rb

```ruby
  def zip_code
    Locales.current.parse_postal_code(@address_text)
  end
end
```

ruby/twits/spec/revisions/locales2.1_spec.rb

```ruby
describe Locales do

  describe Locales::Locale do
    let(:locale) { Locales::Locale.new(/\d{5}/) }

    it "parses postal codes with a regex" do
      locale.parse_postal_code('10121').should == '10121'
    end

    it "returns nil if a postal code cannot be parsed" do
      locale.parse_postal_code('abcde').should be_nil
    end
  end

  it "Uses US Locale by default" do
    Locales.current.should == Locales::UNITED_STATES
  end

  it "can parse 5 digit zip codes" do
    Locales.current.parse_postal_code('zip is 12345').should == '12345'
  end

  it "allows the locale to be changed" do
    Locales.current = Locales::UNITED_KINGDOM
    Locales.current.should == Locales::UNITED_KINGDOM
  end
end
```

ruby/twits/lib/revisions/locales2.1.rb

```ruby
module Locales
  def self.current
    @current || UNITED_STATES
  end

  def self.current=(new_locale)
    @current = new_locale
  end

  class Locale
    def initialize(postal_code_regex)
      @postal_code_regex = postal_code_regex
    end
```

```ruby
    def parse_postal_code(text)
      m = @postal_code_regex.match(text)
      return m[0] if m
    end
  end

  UNITED_STATES = Locale.new(/\d{5}/)
  UNITED_KINGDOM = Locale.new(/[A-Z]{1,2}[0-9R][0-9A-Z]? [0-9][ABD-HJLNP-UW-Z]{2}/)

end
```

Autotest tells us this test passes, but now, suddenly, other tests start to fail—sometimes. Because we're globally changing the state of the application from within this example, tests will now either pass or fail depending on the order that they're run in.

One way to fix this would be to reset the locale back to UNITED_STATES in an after() method on the spec. However, we find that the best way to avoid temporal dependencies like this is to just avoid sharing state between tests. In this case, forgetting to reset the shared state in the Locales class caused problems for all the downstream tests. A better option would have been to mock out the call to Locales.current(), returning the value we needed for the test. That mock would be automatically reset after each test, so we wouldn't have to worry about remembering to clean up the state.

```ruby
ruby/twits/spec/revisions/user2.9_spec.rb
it "uses the current locale to parse zip codes" do
  Locales.should_receive(:current).and_return(Locales::UNITED_KINGDOM);
  user = User.new
  user.address_text = '51-55 Gresham Street, 6th Floor London, England EC2V 7HQ'
  user.zip_code.should == 'EC2V 7HQ'
end
```

Temporal dependencies like this can also indicate a poor design. In this case, the Locales class is acting like a mutable singleton,[5] which in our opinion should generally be avoided. Perhaps we should have each User have its own Locale? In any case, the unreliable test is telling us that we need to reconsider our design because it leads to demonstrably inconsistent behavior.

2.6 Creating an Exhaustive Suite

We write exhaustive specs for all the behavior we care about. If it doesn't matter, however, we don't test for it. While adding too many specs is not as

---

5. See *Design Patterns: Elements of Reusable Object-Oriented Software* [GHJV95] for a definition of the Singleton pattern.

much of a sin as adding too few, there is certainly an optimal amount of testing that ensures correctness without crossing into overspecifying our system with irrelevant conditions.

For example, let's say that we wanted to enhance our zip_code() method to handle nine-digit zip codes. As a first step, we might write a test like this:

ruby/twits/spec/revisions/user2.10_spec.rb
```ruby
it "should extract 9 digit zip codes too" do
  user = User.new
  user.address_text = '1521 Fake St.\nFaketown, MO 12345-6789'
  user.zip_code.should == '12345-6789'
end
```

We can make this new test—and the others we've written—pass with an updated version of our UNITED_STATES locale that looks like this:

ruby/twits/lib/locales.rb
```ruby
UNITED_STATES = Locale.new(/(\d{5})(-\d{4})?/)
```

So our tests pass now. Are we done? Should we add some tests to the Locales spec? What additional tests should we add? As we discussed in *Don't Duplicate Your Design*, on page 19, we don't need to limit ourselves to one test method per production method. We want to ensure all the behavior provided by this method is tested. If that behavior is complex (as regular expressions usually are), then it may take more than one example in our spec to test it all.

In *Test Driven Development: By Example* [Bec02], Kent Beck suggests that you write tests until fear transmutes to boredom. What's scary here? The regular expression is probably a good place to start. Is that ? operator correctly applied to the second group? What happens if it wasn't? Perhaps we need an example for a partial zip code. What if there are two zip codes in the address? Is that possible? Is it likely?

The answers to all of these questions depend on many things: the kind of data you have and how you got them, your comfort level with regular expressions, who will be calling this method and why. There's no one right answer. We want to ensure all valuable behavior is tested, but it's important to write new examples for a specific purpose and not just because there's more stuff we could check.

One great benefit we've found to creating an exhaustive suite of specs is that writing code that's easily testable has a positive effect on our overall design. We find testable code to generally be more decoupled, more cohesive, easier to change, and more intention revealing. In our experience, if a class is well designed, it might be testable, but if it's testable, it's probably well designed. By writing tests for everything we care about, we're helping to create the best designs we can.

Finally, if we're fearful that a change you made might have created code that's untested or just unnecessary, we can do a little detective work to find out. Just delete (or change) the code and make sure a test fails with an informative message. We only need to be sure to do it in a way that doesn't merely create a syntax error. For example, when we moved from using the Test::Unit test to the RSpec spec to test our last_five_tweets() method, we might have missed something. How can we be sure? Let's go back and look for something that we can delete while keeping the code syntactically correct.

ruby/twits/lib/revisions/user2.7.rb
```ruby
require 'twitter'

class User
  attr_accessor :twitter_username

  def last_five_tweets
    return Twitter::Search.new.per_page(5).from(@twitter_username).map do |tweet|
      tweet[:text]
    end.to_a
  end
end
```

Hmm...I wonder what Autotest would tell us if we deleted that call to to_a()?

```
Finished in 0.07231 seconds

5 examples, 0 failures
```

The fact that the specs still passed after we deleted that code means it was untested, even though a code coverage tool would report this code as being 100 percent covered. Perhaps we took too big of a step in our implementation of this method. In any case, map() returns an array already, so calling to_a() is redundant here, and we'll leave it out. If the test had failed, we'd know that to_a() was doing something that affected the behavior of this method (which would have been quite an interesting result)!

2.7 Closing the Loop

So we've seen how creating a FIREy test suite supports the primary feedback loop of continuous testing. Healthy tests give us instant feedback when things break (or when they start to work). Running our tests all the time tells us when they start to get a little crufty and gives us some hints about what to do about it.

Now what?

- Fire up Autotest and go change something in your code. Does a test fail? If not, add more tests until it does, then change your code to the way it was. Does everything pass now?

- Experiment with custom assertion methods and matchers in your examples. See if you can make them more informative by providing additional content. Try to capture the value of the result you're asserting.

- If you haven't tried a behavior driven development framework like RSpec, give it a shot! There are BDD frameworks for almost every language,[6] so no matter what languages you work with, you can start writing executable specs today. Try writing some examples that really read like specifications.

- Are your specs slow? Try running RSpec with the --profile option turned on. This will display the ten slowest specs in your suite and give you a great place to start cleaning things up. If you're not using RSpec, you can still profile your tests using the test_benchmark gem.

- Do your tests fail if run in a different order? Check for shared setup and/or state between tests. Remember that the failing test may not actually be causing the problem.

- While it's not necessary to have 100 percent code coverage, uncovered code represents risk. Run a code coverage tool to get an idea of the trouble areas and poke around a bit.

---

6.   http://en.wikipedia.org/wiki/Behavior_Driven_Development#Tools

CHAPTER 3

Extending Your Environment

Our development environment is the bridge between our ability to solve problems and the digital world where our solutions are manifest. Whether using a commercial IDE or a simple text editor and a well-worn set of bash scripts, we take the time to twist and tweak our environment for each project. We're not looking for "the one true environment" but rather to continuously adapt our tools to the specific problems we're trying to solve.

In the last chapter, we were simply users of Autotest. We just installed it and let it run tests for us, but we didn't really adapt it to our specific needs. In this chapter, we're going to look at how to extend and adapt Autotest to give us feedback beyond passing or failing tests. Because of Ruby's dynamic nature, Autotest forms a very solid foundation for these additional feedback loops. As we'll see, its flexibility allows us to easily extend it to meet our needs with just a few lines of code. Our goal in doing this—as lofty as it may be—is instantaneous verification of every essential behavior or attribute of the systems we build as we build them.

From using plugins to adding event hooks, using metaprogramming with CT, and making your own plugins, there are lots of ways to extend Autotest and create additional feedback loops. We'll look at a few in this chapter.

3.1 Using Autotest Plugins

Autotest has a very flexible plugin system, and there are plenty of plugins out there that will help you run your tests faster and get more feedback. Some of them are clearly better than the default Autotest behavior. Some of them are just different. You should consider which ones are appropriate for you and the kinds of projects you work on. Installing them, as we'll see, is pretty easy.

Using Autotest with Rails

As we discussed in *Is Autotest Really Going to Run ALL of My Tests on Every Change?*, on page 17, Autotest maintains a set of mappings from production files to specs (or tests) and uses them to select which tests to run when changes are made. As we'll see in *Mapping Tests to Resources*, on page 42, it's possible to configure these mappings yourself. When you're working with Rails, however, we don't need to do that because it's already been done for us. By installing the autotest-rails gem, Autotest will automatically detect when we're working in a Rails project and create the appropriate mappings.

What mappings does it create? As of version 4.1.0, it creates the following:

File(s) Changed	Test(s) Run
lib/*.rb	Matching _test.rb in test/unit
test/*.rb	Test that was changed
app/models/*.rb	Matching _test.rb in test/unit
app/helpers/application_helper.rb	All view and functional tests
app/helpers/*_helper.rb	Matching view and functional tests
app/views/*	Matching view and functional tests
app/controllers/*.rb	Matching controller and functional tests
app/views/layouts/*	test/views/layouts_view_test.rb
config/routes.rb	All controller, view, and functional tests
test/test_helper.rb	All unit, controller, view, and functional tests
config/boot.rb	All unit, controller, view, and functional tests
config/environment*.rb	All unit, controller, view, and functional tests
config/database.yml	All unit, controller, view, and functional tests

autotest-rails also adds exceptions for the db, doc, log, public, script, tmp, and vendor directories, so changes to files in those directories will not trigger test runs.

Stop Polling

By default, Autotest polls the filesystem to detect changes to files. If you have a lot of files in your project, this can start to become a heavy load on your CPU. The *autotest-fsevent* plugin for Autotest uses OS X's file system event API to detect changes by event callbacks rather than by polling. This plugin is really easy to use and will definitely save you some time (and save your laptop battery). But first we need to get the gem:

```
$ gem install autotest-fsevent
```

Now we just need to tell Autotest to load this plugin. In this case we always want to have Autotest use fsevent to detect changes, so we're going to create an Autotest configuration file in our home directory called .autotest and add the following:

```
require 'autotest/fsevent'
```

Now Autotest just runs faster. What could be easier? If you're on OS X, this plugin is truly a no-brainer.

Spork

Another great way to speed up your tests is with the *Spork* gem.[1] Spork runs your specs in a server that is spawned in the background, eliminating the environment startup time from your feedback loop. This can be especially valuable on a project with a lot of dependencies, as the additional load time for those dependencies can become noticeable (and unwanted). For an example of how to use Spork to speed up tests in Rails, see Section 5.5, *Running Rails Specs Fast*, on page 86.

Growl Notifications

If you'd rather not keep a terminal window up to run Autotest, there are other options for reporting passing and failing tests visually. The *autotest-growl* plugin uses the OS X event notification app *Growl* to report results. If you're a OS X user, you're probably familiar with the Growl notification application (and if not, you should go get it right now).[2] Just as with the fsevent plugin, we install this as a gem:

```
$ gem install autotest-growl --version=0.2.9
```

We enable this plugin by adding require 'autotest/growl' to our .autotest config file. If we do that for our current project, we get something that looks like the following:

There are other plugins out there as well—this is just a sample. Depending on the kind of project you're working on, you may find yourself using some

---

1. https://github.com/timcharper/spork

2. http://growl.info

or all of them. A quick Google search for "Autotest plugins" is all you need to check out what's new and available.

3.2 Adding Event Hooks

You may have noticed in our example .autotest configuration files that the syntax for adding these plugins is rather familiar. If you haven't guessed already, the "configuration" file for Autotest is just another Ruby file. Autotest includes these files automatically when it starts, and in addition to enabling plugins using require, you can also add snippets of Ruby code to interact with Autotest's API.[3]

One particularly nifty bit of the Autotest API is Autotest::add_hook method. This method accepts a block that will be called whenever a particular event in the Autotest lifecycle occurs. Here are the currently supported events (as of Autotest 4.1.4):

Hook Name	Description
:all_good	Reset a failure related state. Called every time Autotest updates.
:died	Autotest is about to exit with an exception.
:green	All tests pass.
:initialize	Autotest is starting up. *This is great for tweaking Autotest's configuration.*
:interrupt	User has interrupted Autotest (requesting that all tests be rerun).
:quit	Autotest is about to exit at the user's request.
:ran_command	Autotest finished running a batch of tests.
:red	Tests are failing.
:reset	Test history has been reset.
:run_command	Autotest is about to run a batch of tests.
:updated	The list of files to test has been updated.
:waiting	Autotest is waiting for new changes.

Let's take a look at how we can use these hooks to get more and better feedback about the changes we make to our code.

---

3. http://zentest.rubyforge.org/ZenTest/Autotest.html

Watch Out for Broken Hooks

As you work through these examples, you may run into an eccentricity of Autotest related to handling errors in hooks. If your hook handler raises any kind of error, Autotest will fail silently. If, for example, you have a syntax error in a handler like :green or :red, Autotest will exit as soon as it is executed (with no warnings or errors reported). Worse yet, if you have an error in an :initialize handler, Autotest will quit immediately after it starts.

As we'll see in Section 3.3, *Creating Plugins*, on page 45, this is a really good reason to move any nontrivial hook code to an Autotest plugin that can be unit-tested outside of Autotest itself.

Selectively Ignoring Files

As we discussed in the previous chapter, Autotest monitors our project for changes and runs tests in response. But how does it know what files are in our project? Well, it makes a very simple assumption, which is that everything in the directory it started from, or in any subdirectory of that directory, should be examined if it has a known file extension. This often results in many files (in revision control metadata, for example) being included in the search that are not necessary. That can slow down Autotest and, potentially, include tests that aren't really in our project. Thankfully, we can use Autotest's API to add our own filters or exceptions to Autotest's standard list:

```
ruby/twits/.autotest
Autotest.add_hook :initialize do |autotest|
  %w{.git .DS_Store vendor}.each do |exception|
    autotest.add_exception(exception)
  end
  false
end
```

Since it's only called at startup, the :initialize hook is commonly used to configure Autotest, and that's what we're doing here. By adding an exception for the .git directory, we keep Autotest from scanning our local git repository. The .DS_Store entry keeps Autotest away from the file used by OS X to store custom attributes of a directory. Finally, the vendor entry keeps Autotest from watching third-party libraries included in our Rails project. We return false at the end of this block because Autotest will stop processing hooks for a given event if one of them returns true. As our project grows, we'll be on the lookout for new exceptions to add to this list.

Continuous Source Control Integration

Let's say you work on a team that is constantly checking things into source control (a very good thing, in our opinion). With such a rapid rate of change, you might find it difficult to keep your code completely up-to-date. One solution (that we have actually heard someone suggest) is to not check in so many changes. Another, more pragmatic solution would be to have Autotest automatically pull changes from source control whenever we are ready to integrate new changes, that is, every time all of our tests pass. To do this, we'll add a hook to the :green event in our .autotest configuration file, like so:

```
ruby/twits/.autotest
Autotest.add_hook :green do
  Kernel.system('svn up')
  false
end
```

While automatically pulling changes from source control might seem a little scary at first, consider this: if your changes won't conflict with what's in the main repository, what will it hurt? If you want to know what's changed, you can always review the output in the terminal where Autotest is running. On the other hand, if your changes *will* conflict, don't you want to know about it as soon as possible? The longer you let conflicts linger, the worse they tend to get.

We've been working this way for a while. It's actually quite pleasant, and if you try it, you will likely notice that the number of merge conflicts you have to endure quickly drops to near zero. Also, just as the continuous testing feedback loop encourages us to work in small steps and quickly cycle between passing and failing states, this update hook will encourage us to integrate our changes often. After all, if your code is merged, your tests pass, and you don't have any refactoring left to do, why not simply check in?

Mapping Tests to Resources

As we discussed in Section 2.4, *Writing Fast Tests*, on page 23, maintaining a fast test suite is essential to creating a rapid feedback loop. Accessing the filesystem is often a source of test slowness, but it is not inherently bad. As solid state drives become faster and more widely available, we may find that it is possible to write fast tests that access the filesystem. In some cases, it may make sense to push sample data or configuration from tests out to files. If we create these dependencies, however, we must ensure that any changes to those files trigger a test run, or else changing them may silently break our tests.

Let's say that we wrote a spec, named config_spec.rb, to perform some valida-
tions of our Rails configuration files. Of course, there is no matching file for
this test, so Autotest won't know to run this test if we change a file in the
config directory. The add_mapping() method provided by Autotest allows us to
map files to tests like so:

```
ruby/twits/.autotest
Autotest.add_hook :initialize do |autotest|
  autotest.add_mapping %r%^config/.*.rb$% do
    autotest.files_matching(/^config_spec.rb$/)
  end
  false
end
```

Here we're mapping all the Ruby files in the config directory, as mapped by
the regular expression %r%^config/.*.rb$% to our new spec, config_spec.rb. However,
just adding this mapping is not sufficient to make Autotest run our spec
when we change a configuration file. In addition to the file-to-test mappings,
Autotest has a list of exceptions, as we saw in *Selectively Ignoring Files*, on
page 41. Is the config directory included in the list of exceptions? A quick
change to our hook will tell us for sure. Let's add the following to our hook:

```
puts autotest.exceptions
```

Now we can see the list of exceptions that Autotest is configured with. Any
exceptions added by the plugins we have installed (or that have been discovered as we'll see in *Plugin Discovery*, on page 50) will be included in this
list. We restart Autotest to apply this change to our configuration file, which
produces the following:

```
% autospec
(?-mix:config\/|coverage\/|db\/|doc\/|log\/|public\/|script\/|tmp\/|vendor\/
|rails|vendor\/plugins|previous_failures\.txt)
```

Ah ha! There's the config directory. Thankfully, we can remove this exception
from our :initialize as well:

```
ruby/twits/.autotest
Autotest.add_hook :initialize do |autotest|
  autotest.remove_exception 'config/'
  autotest.add_mapping %r%^config/.*.rb$% do
    autotest.files_matching(/^config_spec.rb$/)
  end
  false
end
```

Now any change to our configuration files will result in our spec being run.

Searching for Technical Debt

In order to keep a tight feedback loop going, we often defer coding tasks until all our tests pass. For example, when applying practices like test driven development, we will often create very short-term technical debt in order to get a test to pass. We're just looking for code that works; we don't want to worry too much about design. Once the test passes and our assumptions have been validated, we go back and update the design to reflect our new understanding. Since we take small steps and work with a safety net (our tests), this code never lasts long.

Even so, because this temporary code is sometimes very poorly designed, we want to make sure we don't lose track of it. In some cases, the changes driven out by a single test may open up two or more possible improvements to the design. If you're anything like us, your memory cannot be trusted with information of such importance, so we write ourselves a little comment to remind us to return:

```
# DEBT Remove the duplication between Lead and Opportunity
```

This kind of comment is useless, however, unless you have a mechanism to report it. That's where Autotest comes in:

```
ruby/twits/.autotest
Autotest.add_hook :green do
  Kernel.system('find . -name "*.rb" | xargs grep -n "# DEBT"')
end
```

Here we've just combined a few shell commands to look for debt comments in our code. The find command searches for Ruby files in our project. We then use the | operator to redirect the output of that command to the input of xargs, a very handy tool that invokes another command once for each line that it passed using the contents of that line as the parameter. In this case the command is grep, which we use to search for our special comment. So a new debt comment added to lead.rb would result in the following output from Autotest:

```
./app/models/lead.rb:2:# DEBT remove the duplication between Lead and Opportunity
```

Reporting the existence of these comments in Autotest gives us a single source of information for the state of our code. Instead of maintaining a separate list of things to do somewhere else (text file, notecard, legal pad, etc.), we can track it right in the code and report it along with failing tests. This helps ensure that we won't let this short-term, high-interest debt get out of control and (heaven forbid) accidentally check it in.

Creating Plugins • 45

> ### Debt Comments in Rails
>
> If you're using Rails, check out the *notes* rake task. It scans for commonly used debt comments and prints a summary of them. If you want to use these conventions for tracking technical debt, just call `rake notes` from your Autotest hook instead of using `find` and `grep`.

These are some examples of how to use Autotest hooks to create additional feedback loops. Depending on what kind of project we're working on, we may use them or not. What's essential is that we use these facilities to create appropriate automated feedback loops for whatever project we're working on. We want to stay informed about what our code is doing at all times. People make mistakes. Perhaps better than anything else, that's what we're good at. What we don't want to do is compound those mistakes by making bad decisions based on the outcome of prior bad decisions.

3.3 Creating Plugins

Adding event hooks right to Autotest's configuration file is a great way to add some simple extensions. It's not the most testable environment, however, and once we move beyond simple system calls and Ruby one-liners, we find ourselves wanting to actually write some tests for our extensions. This book is about testing, after all.

In this section, we're going to create a plugin for Autotest that tracks and reports statistics about how often we do various things. These statistics can provide another form of feedback (you knew we were going to say that, didn't you?) about whether or not the changes we make to our development environment have a positive or negative effect. By creating this as a plugin for Autotest, we gain two things:

- We can easily test our extensions once we are decoupled from Autotest.

- We can package our extensions as Ruby gems so that we may share them with others.

Creating a Skeleton

The first thing we need to do is create a gem. In a directory outside of our twits project, we run the following commands:

```
$ jeweler --rspec --gemcutter --create-repo autotest-stats
```

As we saw in Section 2.1, *Getting Started with Autotest*, on page 11, Jeweler makes this easy enough. But we've added some options here because we want to be able to share this plugin as a gem. Using the --create-repo option will tell Jeweler to create a repository on GitHub for our new project. To get this to work, however, we have to tell Jeweler a little information about our GitHub account. It gets this information from a *.gitconfig* file in your home directory. If you do not already have this file, you can create it using your favorite text editor, modeling it after the following template:

```
[user]
    name = YourUserName
    email = YourEmailAddress
[github]
    user = YourUserName
    token = YourGitHubApiToken
```

Of course, if you don't have an account on GitHub or don't want to publish this project to it, you can simply omit the --create-repo option. But why not share when sharing is so easy?

With this one command, Jeweler has created all the configuration files we need to build and publish our gem to the Gemcutter repository. With Jeweler, there really is no excuse not to share your Autotest configuration tweaks with the world.

However, Jeweler doesn't have an --autotest-plugin option (yet!), so we're going to make a few small changes to match the Autotest conventions. First, we're going to rename our main plugin file from autotest-stats.rb to simply stats.rb. We're then going to move it into a directory named autotest under the lib directory. We're also going to rename and move the spec to match this structure so that our project now looks like this:

```
|-autotest-stats
  |-lib
  |---autotest
  |-----stats.rb
  |-spec
  |---spec_helper.rb
  |---autotest
  |-----stats_spec.rb
   .git
  .gitignore
  .rspec
  LICENSE
  README.rdoc
  Rakefile
```

We're going to need to update spec_helper.rb to reflect the fact that the main file in our plugin row resides in lib/autotest:

ruby/autotest-stats/spec/spec_helper.rb
```
require 'autotest/stats'
```

Finally, we need to change the path to our spec helper in stats_spec.rb. Firing up autospec should then give us a starting point (a.k.a. a failing spec):

```
1)
RuntimeError in 'AutotestStats fails'
Hey buddy, maybe you should rename this file and start specing for real
./spec/autotest/stats_spec.rb:5:
```

Right you are.

Hooking In

Now let's add a feature to our newly created plugin. We're going to track how many times the user cycles between red and green states (a rough measure of how many TDD cycles they do in a day). The first thing we're going to want are some hooks to monitor for passing/failing tests. We'll need to add an :initialize hook to set up the initial state for our plugin. After a few test/code iterations, we've added some new examples to our spec:

ruby/autotest-stats/spec/autotest/stats_spec.rb
```
it "should add hooks to autotest" do
  Autotest.should_receive(:add_hook).with(:initialize)
  Autotest.should_receive(:add_hook).with(:red)
  Autotest.should_receive(:add_hook).with(:green)
  require File.expand_path(File.dirname(__FILE__) + '/../../lib/autotest/stats')
end

describe "after Autotest initializes" do

  include Autotest::Stats

  before( :each ) do
    init_hook
  end

  it "should track the number of red/green cycles" do
    @cycles.should == 0
    red_hook
    green_hook
    @cycles.should == 1
  end

  it "should not treat multiple green events as cycles" do
    red_hook
    2.times {green_hook}
    @cycles.should == 1
  end
end
```

Here's the code that satisfies them:

```
ruby/autotest-stats/lib/autotest/stats.rb
require 'rubygems'
require 'autotest'

module Autotest::Stats
  attr_reader :cycles

  Autotest.add_hook(:initialize) { init_hook }
  Autotest.add_hook(:red) { red_hook }
  Autotest.add_hook(:green) { green_hook }

  def init_hook
    @cycles = 0
  end

  def green_hook
    @cycles += 1 if @failing
    @failing = false
  end

  def red_hook
    @failing = true
  end
end
```

And we can even run these specs using autospec:

```
Finished in 0.003103 seconds

3 examples, 0 failures
```

In the first example, the call to require() reloads the file, reexecuting all the statements defined in our Autotest::Stats module. Although this is technically the second time this module has been loaded (the first being when it was loaded by spec_helper.rb), doing it twice has no ill effect and is sufficient to satisfy the test. When we require this file from our .autotest config file, the same process will occur. When the module is loaded by Autotest, our hooks will be added.

Writing specs for these hooks is a bit tricky. Notice that we're just calling out to module level methods from the hooks themselves. Assuming that this wiring is "too simple to fail," then all we need to test are the methods. If you prefer, you can create these handlers as Ruby procs instead and wire them directly into Autotest. We think this reads better though.

No News Is Good News

At this point, we're capturing some statistics, but we never report anything back to the user. To close this feedback loop, we're going to need some kind of notification or report of these data.

We could simply report the number of cycles each time the tests are run. While this would certainly be easy to implement, it wouldn't really be that informative to the user. If I know I've run through sixty cycles today, informing me when I hit sixty-one isn't really all that valuable. This constant stream of mostly irrelevant information would, at best, be ignored. At worst, it would become a distraction.

To address this problem and others like it, we employ the principle "No news is good news" when creating feedback loops. Our goal is to create an environment where we get lots of different kinds of feedback instantaneously. Feedback loops can become problematic if the signal-to-noise ratio is too low.

In this case, we're only going to report individual changes for the first five cycles. After that, we'll report them every five cycles. To do this, we'll need to print something to the console. So we add a new example to our spec:

```ruby
ruby/autotest-stats/spec/autotest/stats_spec.rb
it "should report every cycle up to five" do
  should_receive(:puts).with("1 cycle")
  (2..5).each {|count| should_receive(:puts).with("#{count} cycles")}
  6.times do
    red_hook
    green_hook
  end
end

describe "after five cycles have passed" do
  before( :each ) do
    5.times do
      red_hook
      green_hook
    end
  end

  it "should report every five cycles thereafter" do
    should_not_receive(:puts).with("6 cycles")
    4.times do
      red_hook
      green_hook
    end

    should_receive(:puts).with("10 cycles")
    2.times do
```

```
        red_hook
        green_hook
      end
    end
end
```

And here's the corresponding implementation:

```
ruby/autotest-stats/lib/autotest/stats.rb
def green_hook
  @cycles += 1 if @failing
  @failing = false
  puts "1 cycle" if (@cycles == 1)
  if @cycles.between? 2,5 or @cycles % 5 == 0
    puts "#{@cycles} cycles"
  end
end
```

So when we create feedback loops to enhance our CT environment, we follow the convention that positive results (passing tests, valid syntax, unchanged state, etc.) are not worth mentioning. At most, we would want to report that these things were, in fact, checked, but we don't want to waste any screen real estate reporting that the results were OK. The only thing we generally want to report is when something goes wrong or when something is different. In that case, we want to give ourselves as much information as is necessary to diagnose the problem.

This creates a pleasant and easily consumable rate of information flow (rather than a fire hose). It also creates a sufficiently large contrast between positive and negative states: lots of output means failure, and little to no output means things are OK.

Plugin Discovery

Remember earlier, in Section 2.1, *Getting Started with Autotest*, on page 11, when we set up Autotest? We also installed the autotest-rails plugin, right? We never configured it, though, so how did Autotest know to use it?

Autotest has a plugin discovery mechanism that allows it to automatically enable plugins. It scans through all of your gems to find plugins by searching for a file named autotest/discover.rb. While sometimes very convenient, this can create problems for plugin authors (and even plugin users) who don't understand how it works. Let's take a closer look at how this magic happens in order to demystify this process a little.

When Autotest is started, it will search your loadpath, vendor/plugins, and rubygems for autotest/discover.rb. When it finds that file, it loads it, allowing you to register *discovery* blocks using Autotest.add_discovery(). These blocks are invoked at a very early stage in the Autotest initialization process and allow you to provide a subclass of Autotest that should be used in lieu of the standard one. The block simply needs to return a string, or a list of strings, that corresponds to files that define a subclass of Autotest. These discovery files are very simple. Here's an example from autotest-rails:

```
Autotest.add_discovery do
  "rails" if File.exist? 'config/environment.rb'
end
```

Defining our own subclass to Autotest allows us to add a lot more functionality than what could be added through hooks alone. However, as a plugin author you need to be very careful about what you require() in your discover.rb file. Anything in there will be loaded by Autotest simply if your gem is installed, regardless of whether or not the user has added a require() for your gem to their .autotest config file.

Packaging It Up

So now that we've got our first useful bit of functionality, we're ready to do a release. Jeweler makes this pretty easy, but we have a couple of house-keeping tasks to do first.

First we need to open up the Rakefile in the root of our project and fill in a few things Jeweler couldn't fill in for us. The first is a summary and description of our new plugin gem. Note that depending on which version of Jeweler you're using, you may have to define gem.files to ensure all the files are included.

ruby/autotest-stats/Rakefile
```
Jeweler::Tasks.new do |gem|
  gem.name = "autotest-stats"

  # Filled in the summary and description for our new plugin
  gem.summary = %Q{Collects and reports statistics about how you write tests}
  gem.description = %Q{An autotest plugin that monitors how you write tests
    and reports interesting statistics as you work}

  #Adding ZenTest as a dependency
  gem.add_dependency "ZenTest", ">= 4.1.0"
  gem.files = FileList["[A-Z]*.*", "{lib,spec}/**/*"]
```

Now we're ready to install our gem and try it out.

```
$ rake install
```

Now we can just add require 'autotest/stats' to the .autotest file in our home directory to enable our new plugin. At this point, assuming you've created an
account, pushing a release to Gemcutter is as easy as this:

```
$ gem push
```

Check out http://gemcutter.org for more details.

3.4   Closing the Loop

In this chapter, we've shown some ways to use Autotest as a platform for
creating new feedback loops in your development environment. By adding
your own custom Autotest hooks or by using or creating plugins, you can
automatically and immediately verify almost any aspect of your system. We
covered just a few of the aspects you might want to test, but there are many
more. Think about what the requirements of your project are and if there
are ways to verify them faster.

Now what?

- Try checking for bad code using *Flog* for complexity,[4] *Reek* for code
  smells,[5] or *Flay* for duplication.[6]

- Check code coverage automatically after all tests pass using rcov.[7]

- Make a plugin to scan development logs for unexpected problems. This
  can be a great alternative to simply tailing log files as you use your app.

---

4.   http://github.com/seattlerb/flog
5.   http://github.com/kevinrutherford/reek
6.   http://github.com/seattlerb/flay
7.   https://github.com/relevance/rcov

CHAPTER 4

Interacting with Your Code

Reading code is good, but nothing beats experimentation. However well you think you know a language or library, the cold, hard reality of tested behavior trumps all.

That's why we really like to run code and see what it does with exploratory tests, rather than speculate about what it might or might not do. We generally prefer this method to looking up behavior in documentation because documentation can be incorrect. Better still, an exploratory test can ensure that if the behavior provided by the library changes in the future, we'll have an automated way to find out about it. We don't leave those tests in our code all the time—only when there's a specific risk or problem that we're trying to mitigate—but when we need them, boy, are they helpful.

In this chapter, we're going to discuss how interacting with your code, rather than merely reading or executing it, can be a powerful technique that is made much easier with continuous testing.

4.1 Understanding Code by Changing It

When running tests continuously, the easiest way to learn what code does is often just to change it and see what happens. In contrast to running an external tool like a debugger or only reading through the code, when you test it continuously you can modify it in a way that proves (or disproves) your theory about what is going on and let the test runner react to your change. In the previous chapter, for example, we looked at how temporarily deleting code can help us determine if it is unnecessary. Let's look at how this technique can help us answer other kinds of questions we may have about our code.

Are We Testing This?

How can we check whether particular conditions in our code are tested? How can we be sure, for example, that we're testing a method like zip_code() with a nil address? Because RSpec adds should() and should_not() methods to Object when running specs, we can temporarily add assertions to our production code to check whether or not particular cases are being tested. So we can answer our question by making a small change to zip_code():

ruby/twits/lib/revisions/user3.1.rb
```
def zip_code
  @address_text.should_not == nil
  Locales.current.parse_postal_code(@address_text)
end
```

If all our tests pass after adding such an assertion, we know that case is *not* being tested. After saving this change, Autotest immediately runs our tests and tell us that, in fact, we never test zip_code() with a nil value. To cover this condition, we can leave the assertion in place and then add a test that we expect to fail at that point:

ruby/twits/spec/revisions/user3.1_spec_fail.rb
```
it "should treat missing addresses like missing zip code" do
  user = User.new
  user.zip_code.should == nil
end
```

A quick save, and Autotest reveals that we're now covering that condition:

```
F

Failures:

  1) Twitter User should treat missing addresses like missing zip code
     Failure/Error: user.zip_code.should be nil
       expected not: == nil
               got:    nil
     # ./code/ruby/twits/lib/revisions/user3.1.rb:8:in `zip_code'
     # ./code/ruby/twits/spec/revisions/user3.1_spec_fail.rb:8:in
`block (2 levels) in <top (required)>'

Finished in 0.00105 seconds
1 example, 1 failure
```

Now we can remove the assertion in User and let the example run normally:

```
8 examples, 0 failures
```

So it turns out that case works without any additional changes. If the test had failed, we would know that the current implementation couldn't handle a nil address, and we could change it as necessary. Also note that before we added this example, the zip_code() method was completely covered. Unlike the previous example, where the code was merely being executed but not tested, in this case all the existing code is being tested. What is missing is a particular usage of that code (and what the expected behavior should be).

We refer to these kinds of assertions, added to production code rather than tests, as *inline assertions*. By temporarily adding these kinds of assertions to our code, we get an immediate, reliable verification of whether or not this condition is tested. While reading through specs is a great way to learn what your system does (and doesn't do), making them fail is even better.

How Did I Get to This Method?

Ruby's Kernel#caller() method returns a trace of the current call stack. This information can be really useful when trying to figure out how a particular method is used. Say you're staring at a piece of code (for example, the zip_code() method in our user class) and you want to know which tests it's covered by, you can simply add puts caller.first, save the change, and Autotest will report the callers like this:

```
../lib/revisions/user_spec.rb:27
../lib/revisions/user_spec.rb:34
../lib/revisions/user_spec.rb:41
../lib/revisions/user_spec.rb:48
```

These refer to the four lines in our spec where we're calling zip_code(). If this method was being tested indirectly, then we would see entries in this list that weren't specs. In that case, we might want to look three calls back using something like puts caller[0..3].

What Can I Do with This Object?

In a statically typed language, behavior and type are nearly inseparable. If you know an object's type, you know everything that it's capable of doing. In a dynamic language like Ruby, that's not really true. Methods can be added, changed, or removed at runtime, so simply knowing an object's type doesn't necessarily tell you what behaviors it has.

The problem is, we don't always know how to invoke the exact behavior we're looking for. You might know you need to split a string, but what are your options for providing a delimiter? Maybe you're not even sure what the behavior is, but you have a general idea and you just want to know what your options are. No problem, just make a simple call:

```
puts user.zip_code.methods
```

Inline Assertions vs. Assert Keywords

Many languages support an assert keyword that lets you check for particular conditions in your code and raise an error if one of the checks fails. Typically, these kinds of assertions are enabled during testing but turned off in production.

We've never really understood the rationale behind this. Either something is broken or it isn't. Most of the time, if something is broken, we want our code to stop executing as quickly as possible so we don't corrupt data or give the user an erroneous result. The remainder of the time, we want to recover gracefully. That graceful recovery is expected behavior that we want to verify. Failing loud and fast in "test mode" while silently ignoring problems in production just seems crazy.

The intent behind inline assertions differs from these kinds of language-supported assert keywords. Inline assertions are temporary and only used to drive out missing cases in your tests. Once those cases are tested, we remove the inline assertions. Inline assertions may also check for cases that are legitimate—even expected—while assert keywords are only used to check for things that indicate an error state.

This tells us exactly what the object can do. Just like the caller information in the previous example, by temporarily adding this to our code, we can get Autotest to print the list of available methods for each object instance driven out by a particular example. This includes methods dynamically mixed in with Ruby's extend method. If we want to be more discerning about the type of methods we're looking for, we filter the results with a regular expression:

```
puts user.zip_code.methods.grep(/each/)
```

This would tell us all the method names that contain the word each, such as each(), each_byte(), and reverse_each().

Adding Diagnostic Methods

Being a dynamic language with rich metaprogramming support, Ruby allows us to change almost anything in our environment. Not only can we dynamically create new methods and classes, but we can also change any existing method or class based on the particular context in which we're using the system.

We can take advantage of this to add additional diagnostic tools that are available when running specs from Autotest. This gives us a lot of power and control over the kinds of information we can get from our code without cluttering it up with a bunch of logging statements that are only useful when running tests.

> \\//   **Joe asks:**
> ₹ᵒᶠ   # What Is Metaprogramming?
>
> Metaprogramming is writing code that modifies code. In Ruby this can be done in a number of different ways, ranging from calling the extend() or include() methods to add methods to a class or object to simply defining (or redefining) a method for a third-party class in your source code. As one might expect, metaprogramming can cause some rather counterintuitive behavior if not used carefully, but it is a very effective way to change the behavior of existing code without modifying the source itself.

In the previous section, we took advantage of Ruby's built-in methods and the assertion methods mixed in by RSpec to either print information to the console or to intentionally fail a test to indicate what the code was doing. We chose to use these methods mostly because they were already there and we could make use of them.

However, there's no reason to limit ourselves to what's provided. With Ruby, we can add whatever methods we want to whatever classes we want. Let's take our original example:

```
puts user.zip_code.methods.grep(/each/)
```

This is handy but a little more verbose than we'd like, especially considering we're going to delete this code as soon as we find the method we're looking for. What if we could get the same effect by doing this:

```
zip_code.put_methods /each/
```

We can add this method to every object when (and only when) our tests are run just by using Ruby's metaprogramming facilities. First, let's open the spec_helper.rb file in the spec and add our put_methods() method to Ruby's Object:

ruby/twits/spec/spec_helper.rb
```
class Object
  def put_methods(regex=/.*/)
    puts self.methods.grep(regex)
  end
end
```

What we're doing here is dynamically adding a method (put_methods()) to Ruby's base object (Object). This means put_methods() will be available on every object instance in our system whenever this code is loaded in the runtime environment. Now, if we want to know what looping methods are available on a user's zip code, we can find out like so:

```
user.zip_code.put_methods /each/
```

This results in the following output from Autotest:

```
each_cons
each_with_object
each_with_index
each_line
each
each_byte
reverse_each
each_char
each_slice
```

There are many other places we could take this. We could use this technique to look at state within our domain objects by creating custom inspectors for more complex types. This is sometimes preferable to overriding to_s() in our classes when the only motivation for doing so is inspection while running tests.

4.2 Comparing Execution Paths

As we saw in *Are We Testing This?*, on page 54, inline assertions are a powerful way to diagnose what our code is doing as it's being exercised by tests. You can often get the same effect while using a debugger, albeit more slowly. One thing that most debuggers *can't* do, however, is compare multiple paths of execution at the same time.

Take a look at Figure 3, *Debugging vs. interacting with code*, on page 59. Notice how a debugger only allows us to examine one execution path—one call stack, as we show in the example. With a flexible continuous testing environment (like the one we've created), we can run our tests and quickly compare the behavior of our application across different paths. This allows us to experiment not only on the "happy path" through our code but on all the possible paths we've thought of thus far and thereby learn much more about our code than would be possible by merely stepping through it.

If you think about it, this is a much more natural and realistic way to look at code. Unless the programs we write have no branches or loops, there is no single path though the code. In this section, we're going to try looking at our code another way, one that tries to capture what's really going on when our code is running in a production environment.

We can take advantage of our CT environment to help us compare different paths of execution through the code.

Debugging

Interacting

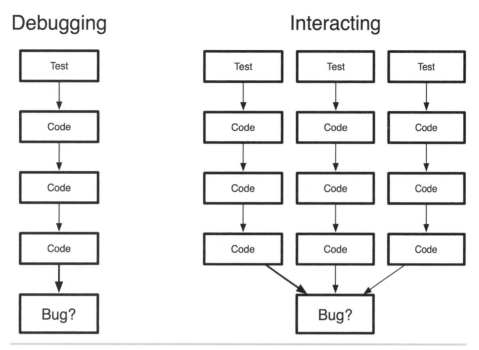

Figure 3—Debugging vs. interacting with code

Comparing Objects

When working a statically typed object-oriented language, the kinds of objects you can pass to a method are generally enforced by the type system. The behaviors that those objects are required to have is generally known because the language itself enforces it.

When working in a dynamically typed language like Ruby, these constraints are lifted. Objects have types, of course, but those types are not used to check the available behaviors of an object. Ruby developers, therefore, are less worried about the type of an object and more worried about what it can do. So long as it "walks like a duck" and our tests pass, it's all good.

However, this can sometimes make reading code rather confusing. This is particularly problematic when trying to add new behavior to an existing method. Because incoming objects are only required to have the essential behaviors they need, we don't know what additional behaviors may be available. The tests have this information at least indirectly, but unless we want to step through with a debugger for every test in our suite, we won't really know for sure what's there.

Let's say that we had a method on our User class named following_me(). This method returns an array of usernames for people who are following the user identified by the instance. As a parameter, it takes users, but it's not clear to us whether this is a collection of usernames, user objects, or something else. It might not even be an array at all; it might be a hash of names to objects or perhaps a graph of User objects.

If all we're trying to do is understand what this code currently does, this isn't really a problem. But let's say we want to enhance the following_me() method, perhaps to sort the returned list of users by some ranking. We'd really like to know what kind of objects we're currently passing to following_me() so that we know what kind of behavior to expect from the incoming collection of users.

To solve this problem, we're going to make a utility module in our spec_helper.rb file named Compare. It's going to do the work of comparing objects across execution paths (in this case, the parameter passed to the following_me() method). We can add a bunch of different comparison methods to this module. In this case, we're going to start with type(). To see the result of the comparison, we can also create a report() method:

```
ruby/twits/spec/spec_helper.rb
module Compare
  def self.type(obj)
    @objects ||= []
    @objects << obj
  end

  def self.report
    puts "Object Types: #{@objects.collect{|o| o.class}.join(', ')}" if @objects
  end
end
```

This looks good, but who's going to call the report() function? Thankfully, RSpec can be configured to run blocks of code before and after the entire test suite is finished. In our case, we want to add an after(:suite) block to allow us to report the results of the comparison once all the tests have been run:

```
ruby/twits/spec/spec_helper.rb
RSpec.configure do |config|
  config.after(:suite) do
    Compare.report
  end
end
```

Now we add our comparison call to following_me():

ruby/twits/lib/revisions/user3.3.rb
```ruby
class User
  attr_accessor :twitter_username, :address_text, :followers

  #...

  def following_me(users={})
    Compare.type(users)
    return @followers if users.empty?
    (@followers || []) & users
  end
end
```

Saving the change instantly yields our results:

```
Finished in 0.04028 seconds

18 examples, 0 failures
Object Types: Array, Array, Hash
```

It can seem like we've been using this method inconsistently. Some callers pass in an Array; another one passes in a Hash (or, perhaps, doesn't pass anything at all!). This works, however, because both of those objects provide the necessary behavior—the power of dynamic typing at work! Now we know that we're going to have to handle both arrays and hashes in order to add any new behavior to this method. And now that we have our comparison methods written, we can use them anywhere to quickly compare objects in different execution paths.

4.3 Learning APIs Interactively

Test driven development is a powerful technique for creating (and modifying) APIs. By using the interface as it is created, subtle usability and behavioral issues can be driven out very quickly. Continuous testing can help us stay on track as we evolve our API, making sure we don't spend any time chasing a solution that won't pass our tests. In this section, we're going to use continuous testing to help us create a class for analyzing the tweets of our users. We'll see how CT tightens the feedback loop and keeps our changes small and steady. We'll also refactor our API a little and see how CT can make that process easier as well.

Tweet Analysis

Our first step, as always, is to describe the behavior that we want:

```
ruby/twits/spec/revisions/tweet_analyzer4.1_spec_fail.rb
describe TweetAnalyzer do
  it "finds the frequency of words in a user's tweets" do
    analyzer = TweetAnalyzer.new(mock_user = double("user"))
    histogram = analyzer.word_frequency()
  end
end
```

When we save, Autotest tells us this test is failing, which is enough to drive the creation of the TweetAnalyzer class:

```
ruby/twits/lib/revisions/tweet_analyzer4.1.rb
class TweetAnalyzer
  def initialize(user)
    @user = user
  end
end
```

Now we can hop back to the spec and add some expectations:

```
ruby/twits/spec/revisions/tweet_analyzer4.2_spec.rb
describe TweetAnalyzer do
  it "finds the frequency of words in a user's tweets" do
    analyzer = TweetAnalyzer.new(mock_user = double("user"))
    histogram = analyzer.word_frequency()
    histogram["one"].should == 1
  end
end
```

Again, a failing test in Autotest tells us we've got work to do in TweetAnalyzer, so we'll fill in just enough implementation to make that pass:

```
ruby/twits/lib/revisions/tweet_analyzer4.2.rb
class TweetAnalyzer
  def initialize(user)
    @user = user
  end

  def word_frequency
    { "one" => 1 }
  end
end
```

We want to maintain a quick feedback loop here. Not only does this mean writing tests that run quickly, but it also means tackling one decision at a time and then validating it. Here, we just want to confirm that passing this information back as a hash will work as expected, so we hardcoded one with specific values just to get back to a green state. We'll specify more realistic behavior in this class with the next test.

Now we'll add a test to specify how we query the tweets from the user:

```ruby
describe TweetAnalyzer do
  it "finds the frequency of words in a user's tweets" do
    analyzer = TweetAnalyzer.new(mock_user = double("user"))
    histogram = analyzer.word_frequency()
    histogram["one"].should == 1
  end

  it "asks the users for recent tweets" do
    analyzer = TweetAnalyzer.new(mock_user = double("user"))
    expected_tweets = ["one too", "too"]
    mock_user.should_receive(:recent_tweets).and_return expected_tweets

    histogram = analyzer.word_frequency()

    histogram["too"].should == 2
  end
end
```

And the failing test leads us to add the corresponding implementation:

```ruby
class TweetAnalyzer
  def initialize(user)
    @user = user
  end

  def word_frequency
    frequency = Hash.new { 0 }
    @user.recent_tweets.each do |tweet|
      tweet.split(/\s/).each do |word|
        frequency[word] += 1
      end
    end
    frequency
  end
end
```

```
F.

Failures:

  1) TweetAnalyzer finds the frequency of words in a user's tweets
     Failure/Error: histogram = analyzer.word_frequency()
       Double "user" received unexpected message :recent_tweets with
(no args)
     # ./code/ruby/twits/lib/revisions/tweet_analyzer4.3.rb:8:in
`word_frequency'
     #
```

```
./code/ruby/twits/spec/revisions/tweet_analyzer4.3_spec_fail.rb:8:in
`block (2 levels) in <top (required)>'

Finished in 0.00077 seconds
2 examples, 1 failure
```

Our new test passes, but as we can see by the failing test, we've created some duplication here. This test used to pass, but when we saved this file, Autotest ran the spec, pointing out the inconsistency between the way we're setting up the user mock in the two examples. This is as quickly as we could have gotten this information, and it's exactly the kind of rapid feedback we want from our CT environment.

To get this test to pass again, we can pull this up into a before() method in the spec and then delete the duplicated code:

ruby/twits/spec/revisions/tweet_analyzer4.4_spec.rb
```ruby
describe TweetAnalyzer do
  before( :each ) do
    @expected_tweets = []
    @mock_user = double('mock user')
    @mock_user.stub(:recent_tweets).and_return @expected_tweets
    @mock_user.stub(:username).and_return("bill")
    @analyzer = TweetAnalyzer.new(@mock_user)
  end

  it "finds the frequency of words in a user's tweets" do
    @expected_tweets << "one"
    histogram = @analyzer.word_frequency()
    histogram["one"].should == 1
  end

  it "asks the users for recent tweets" do
    @expected_tweets << "one two" << "two"
    histogram = @analyzer.word_frequency()
    histogram["two"].should == 2
  end
end
```

The test passes, and Autotest runs all our specs to make sure nothing else is broken:

```
..........

Finished in 0.007493 seconds

10 examples, 0 failures
```

Scaling Up

Twitter limits the number of API calls a single client can make per hour, and it will only give you twenty tweets per request. At this point, we're starting to be concerned about hitting those limits. Every time we call the word_frequency() method, it's going to ask the user for its tweets, which in turn is going to query Twitter (as we saw in *Introducing IO*, on page 23). As we start doing a lot of analysis, the calls to the Twitter API may start being denied because we're calling it too much.

To work around this problem, we're going store previously retrieved tweets in a NOSQL database called MongoDB[1] to store some of the data we're getting back from Twitter. Since this data isn't really relational, it doesn't make sense to put it in a relational database. But we need something more than a key/value store to organize it since we need to query for a specific range of tweets. In our case, we may want to be able to search for a specific number of tweets sorted by timestamp.

However, we've never used this kind of database before, so we're not really sure how to mock out the interaction. Therefore, we're going to take a slightly different approach when writing these tests: we're going to write them *interactively*. That is, we're going to write the tests to learn what behavior we want while still being able to quickly capture that behavior in a test once we've discovered it.

We want to be able to pass in the number of tweets to analyze to the word_frequency() method so that we can control which tweets are fetched from the cache and which are pulled from Twitter. Of course, it starts with a test:

ruby/twits/spec/revisions/tweet_analyzer4.5_spec_fail.rb
```ruby
describe TweetAnalyzer do
  before( :each ) do
    @expected_tweets = []
    @mock_user = double('mock user')
    @mock_user.stub(:recent_tweets).and_return @expected_tweets
    @mock_user.stub(:username).and_return("bill")
    @analyzer = TweetAnalyzer.new(@mock_user)
  end

  it "finds the frequency of words in a user's tweets" do
    @expected_tweets << "one"
    histogram = @analyzer.word_frequency()
    histogram["one"].should == 1
  end
end
```

---

1. http://www.mongodb.org

```
it "asks the users for recent tweets" do
  @expected_tweets << "one two" << "two"
  histogram = @analyzer.word_frequency()
  histogram["two"].should == 2
end

it "can find word frequency for a number of tweets" do
  @expected_tweets << "one" << "two two" << "three three three"
  histogram = @analyzer.word_frequency(3)
  histogram["one"] = 1
  histogram["two"] = 2
  histogram["three"] = 3
end
end
```

If we save this, Autotest tells us it fails, because we haven't added the parameter to word_frequency() yet:

```
..F

Failures:

  1) TweetAnalyzer can find word frequency for a number of tweets
     Failure/Error: histogram = @analyzer.word_frequency(3)
     ArgumentError:
       wrong number of arguments (1 for 0)
     # ./code/ruby/twits/lib/revisions/tweet_analyzer4.3.rb:6:in
`word_frequency'
     #
./code/ruby/twits/spec/revisions/tweet_analyzer4.5_spec_fail.rb:28:in
`block (2 levels) in <top (required)>'

Finished in 0.00243 seconds
3 examples, 1 failure
```

So let's add that method parameter:

```
ruby/twits/lib/revisions/tweet_analyzer4.5.rb
class TweetAnalyzer
  def initialize(user)
    @user = user
  end

  def word_frequency(tweet_count)
    frequency = Hash.new { 0 }
    @user.recent_tweets(tweet_count).each do |tweet|
      tweet.split(/\s/).each do |word|
        frequency[word] += 1
      end
    end
```

```
      frequency
    end
end
```

And save to confirm that the test passes:

```
FF.

Failures:

  1) TweetAnalyzer finds the frequency of words in a user's tweets
     Failure/Error: histogram = @analyzer.word_frequency()
     ArgumentError:
       wrong number of arguments (0 for 1)
     # ./code/ruby/twits/lib/revisions/tweet_analyzer4.5.rb:6:in
`word_frequency'
     #
./code/ruby/twits/spec/revisions/tweet_analyzer4.6_spec_fail.rb:16:in
`block (2 levels) in <top (required)>'

  2) TweetAnalyzer asks the users for recent tweets
     Failure/Error: histogram = @analyzer.word_frequency()
     ArgumentError:
       wrong number of arguments (0 for 1)
     # ./code/ruby/twits/lib/revisions/tweet_analyzer4.5.rb:6:in
`word_frequency'
     #
./code/ruby/twits/spec/revisions/tweet_analyzer4.6_spec_fail.rb:22:in
`block (2 levels) in <top (required)>'

Finished in 0.01047 seconds
3 examples, 2 failures
```

Hmm...our new test passed as we expected, but now our two other tests are breaking. They weren't expecting this method to need a parameter, but the new behavior requires that this method be parameterized. Thankfully, our CT runner helped us catch this inconsistency, so the fix is easy enough:

ruby/twits/lib/revisions/tweet_analyzer4.6.rb
```
class TweetAnalyzer
  def initialize(user)
    @user = user
  end

  def word_frequency(tweet_count=5)
    frequency = Hash.new { 0 }
    @user.recent_tweets(tweet_count).each do |tweet|
      tweet.split(/\s/).each do |word|
        frequency[word] += 1
      end
    end
```

```
      frequency
    end
  end
end
```

At this point, we've made the basic API changes necessary to support caching in the TweetAnalyzer. We're now passing in a variable number of tweets to be analyzed, which is when caching really comes into play. In the next section, we'll see how continuous testing can help us quickly understand the details of how the Ruby Mongo API works in a way that lets us capture our understanding in code and tests.

4.4 Making It till You Fake It

As we saw in Section 2.4, *Writing Fast Tests*, on page 23, dependencies on external services or sources of data can make our tests slow and brittle. But we don't want to mock out these interactions in a vacuum. We want to make sure that when we break these dependencies, we're doing so in a realistic way.

By running our tests continuously against a real service and then mocking out the interactions bit-by-bit (using the real data as a guide), we can break dependencies while ensuring that our tests simulate exactly what will happen in production.

Connecting to MongoDB

In Section 4.3, *Learning APIs Interactively*, on page 61, our goal was to make incremental changes to our API to allow us to cache tweets using MongoDB. Now that we've finished those changes, let's write a test that queries for a lot of tweets to help specify how we'll use our MongoDB cache:

ruby/twits/spec/revisions/tweet_analyzer4.7_spec.rb
```
it "caches tweets in Twitter to prevent multiple requests" do
  cached_tweets = []
  20.times { |i| @queried_tweets << "remote #{i}" }
  20.times { |i| cached_tweets << "cached #{i}" }

  histogram = @analyzer.word_frequency(40)

  histogram["remote"].should == 20
  histogram["cached"].should == 20
end
```

Notice that we changed the name of expected_tweets to queried_tweets to emphasize the point that these tweets are being queried for. Also notice that the cached_tweets variable isn't used in this test (yet). That's because although we have an expectation of what the cached tweets are and what the resulting histogram should look like, we don't yet know enough about how MongoDB works to know how to inject those values into our mock. It's enough to make a failing test though. We can make it pass with this implementation:

```ruby
ruby/twits/lib/revisions/tweet_analyzer4.7.rb
class TweetAnalyzer
  def initialize(user)
    @user = user
  end

  def word_frequency(tweet_count=5)
    frequency = Hash.new { 0 }
    all_tweets = @user.recent_tweets(tweet_count) + cached_tweets
    all_tweets.each do |tweet|
      tweet.split(/\s/).each do |word|
        frequency[word] += 1
      end
    end
    frequency
  end

  def cached_tweets
    (1..20).collect {|i| "cached #{i}" }
  end
end
```

This implementation is simplistic, but it will do for now. At this point, our goal is to understand more about how to get data out of, and put data into, a Mongo database. First, we'll have to check if we have the MongoDB Ruby driver gem installed by adding require 'mongo' to tweet_analyzer.rb:

```ruby
ruby/twits/lib/revisions/tweet_analyzer4.8.rb
require 'mongo'

class TweetAnalyzer
  #...
```

A quick save...

```
/Users/brady/workspace/twits/spec/../lib/tweet_analyzer.rb:1:in
    `require': no such file to load -- mongo (LoadError)
        from /Users/brady/workspace/twits/spec/../lib/tweet_analyzer.rb:1
        from /Users/brady/workspace/twits/spec/../lib/twits.rb:2:in `require'
```

and Autotest tells us that we need to install it.[2] That's easy enough. Just as with the Twitter gem we installed earlier, we just need to add this dependency to our Gemfile:

---

2. You may also need to add require 'rubygems' here, if you haven't already added it somewhere else.

```
ruby/twits/Gemfile
gem 'mongo', "1.2.0"
gem 'bson_ext', "1.2.0"
```

We've also included the *bson_ext* gem, as recommended by the Mongo gem developers. Now we need to fire up the mongodb instance we downloaded from http://mongodb.org:[3]

```
$ mkdir /tmp/db
$ ./bin/mongod --dbpath=/tmp/db
```

Now we're going to add a bit of code to our test to try to use Autotest to quickly add this data to a MongoDB collection and confirm that it is there. We'll start with an assertion:

```
ruby/twits/spec/revisions/tweet_analyzer4.8_spec_fail.rb
it "caches tweets in Twitter to prevent multiple requests" do
  cached_tweets = []
  20.times { |i| @queried_tweets << "remote #{i}" }
  20.times { |i| cached_tweets << "cached #{i}" }

  coll = Mongo::Connection.new.db("twitterCache").collection("bill")
  coll.count().should == 20
  histogram = @analyzer.word_frequency(40)

  histogram["remote"].should == 20
  histogram["cached"].should == 20
end
```

We save, and Autotest tells us we understood the MongoDB docs correctly:

```
...F

Failures:

  1) TweetAnalyzer caches tweets in Twitter to prevent multiple requests
     Failure/Error: coll =
Mongo::Connection.new.db("twitterCache").collection("bill")
     Mongo::ConnectionFailure:
        Failed to connect to a master node at localhost:27017
     #
./code/ruby/twits/spec/revisions/tweet_analyzer4.8_spec_fail.rb:39:in
`new'
     #
./code/ruby/twits/spec/revisions/tweet_analyzer4.8_spec_fail.rb:39:in
`block (2 levels) in <top (required)>'

Finished in 0.01307 seconds
4 examples, 1 failure
```

---

3. Check out http://www.mongodb.org/display/DOCS/Quickstart for more information.

Now that we have a failing test, we can add a bit of code to write our cached tweets to the database. We want to insert the tweets with a timestamp for later analysis. This code is only temporary, and we will run it only once. But once will be enough. If you accidentally hit save twice, it's no big deal! Just call coll.remove() and try again.

```ruby
ruby/twits/spec/revisions/tweet_analyzer4.9_spec.rb
it "caches tweets in Twitter to prevent multiple requests" do
  cached_tweets = []
  20.times { |i| @queried_tweets << "remote #{i}" }
  20.times { |i| cached_tweets << "cached #{i}" }

  coll = Mongo::Connection.new.db("twitterCache").collection("bill")
  cached_tweets.each_with_index { |tweet, index|
    coll.insert({:timestamp => index, :tweet => tweet})
  }
  coll.count().should == 20
  histogram = @analyzer.word_frequency(40)

  histogram["remote"].should == 20
  histogram["cached"].should == 20
end
```

The test passes. We can now delete the code doing the insert, and the test should still pass:

```ruby
ruby/twits/spec/revisions/tweet_analyzer4.10_spec.rb
it "caches tweets in twitter to prevent multiple requests" do
  cached_tweets = []
  20.times { |i| @queried_tweets << "remote #{i}" }
  20.times { |i| cached_tweets << "cached #{i}" }

  coll = Mongo::Connection.new.db("twitterCache").collection("bill")
  coll.count().should == 20
  histogram = @analyzer.word_frequency(40)

  histogram["remote"].should == 20
  histogram["cached"].should == 20
end
```

A quick save, and Autotest tells us that our test data is now in the database with a passing test. At this point, we can expand the assertion a bit to understand more about how to query for documents in MongoDB:

```ruby
ruby/twits/spec/revisions/tweet_analyzer4.11_spec.rb
it "caches tweets in Twitter to prevent multiple requests" do
  cached_tweets = []
  20.times { |i| @queried_tweets << "remote #{i}" }
  20.times { |i| cached_tweets << "cached #{i}" }

  coll = Mongo::Connection.new.db("twitterCache").collection("bill")
  coll.count().should == 20
```

```
actual_tweets = coll.find().collect{|doc| doc['tweet']}
cached_tweets.should == actual_tweets

histogram = @analyzer.word_frequency(40)

histogram["remote"].should == 20
histogram["cached"].should == 20
end
```

Now we can move this code into tweet_analyzer.rb and replace our fake implementation of cached_tweets() with a real one:

ruby/twits/lib/tweet_analyzer.rb
```
def cached_tweets
  coll = Mongo::Connection.new.db("twitterCache").collection(@user.username)
  coll.find().collect{|doc| doc['tweet']}
end
```

And here's our test, now with all the temporary code removed:

ruby/twits/spec/revisions/tweet_analyzer4.12_spec.rb
```
it "caches tweets in Twitter to prevent multiple requests" do
  20.times { |i| @queried_tweets << "remote #{i}" }

  histogram = @analyzer.word_frequency(40)
  histogram["remote"].should == 20
  histogram["cached"].should == 20
end
```

Bringing the "Fake" Back

So this test passes, but while we used the cached tweets to seed our database, we're still not using it in an assertion or expectation. Furthermore, this test relies on a running database instance to pass, and we deleted the code to populate that database a while back. As we saw in Section 2.5, *Writing Reliable Tests*, on page 27, isolating tests from external resources like databases is essential to creating reliable tests. So this dependence on MongoDB is only temporary. Our goal now is to mock out the current behavior of the MongoDB driver, confident that this code works as we expect:

ruby/twits/spec/revisions/tweet_analyzer4.13_spec_fail.rb
```
it "caches tweets in Twitter to prevent multiple requests" do
  20.times { |i| @queried_tweets << "remote #{i}" }
  Mongo::Connection.should_receive(:new).
    and_return(mock_connection = double("connection"))
  mock_connection.should_receive(:db).with("twitterCache").
    and_return(mock_db = double("db"))
  mock_db.should_receive(:collection).with("bill").
    and_return(mock_collection = double("collection"))

  tweet_docs = (0..19).map {|i| {'tweet' => "cached #{i}"}}
  mock_collection.should_receive(:find).and_return tweet_docs
```

```
histogram = @analyzer.word_frequency(40)
histogram["remote"].should == 20
histogram["cached"].should == 20
end
```

It's probable that other examples in this spec indirectly invoke the cached_tweets() method. They happen to pass now because we still have our Mongo instance running. If we stop it and resave tweet_analyzer_spec.rb to trigger a test run, we see that our assumptions are correct:

```
FFF.

Failures:

  1) TweetAnalyzer finds the frequency of words in a user's tweets
     Failure/Error: histogram = @analyzer.word_frequency(3)
     Mongo::ConnectionFailure:
       Failed to connect to a master node at localhost:27017
     # ./code/ruby/twits/lib/tweet_analyzer.rb:22:in `new'
     # ./code/ruby/twits/lib/tweet_analyzer.rb:22:in `cached_tweets'
     # ./code/ruby/twits/lib/tweet_analyzer.rb:11:in `word_frequency'
     #
./code/ruby/twits/spec/revisions/tweet_analyzer4.13_spec_fail.rb:15:in
 `block (2 levels) in <top (required)>'

  2) TweetAnalyzer asks the users for recent tweets
     Failure/Error: histogram = @analyzer.word_frequency()
     Mongo::ConnectionFailure:
       Failed to connect to a master node at localhost:27017
     # ./code/ruby/twits/lib/tweet_analyzer.rb:22:in `new'
     # ./code/ruby/twits/lib/tweet_analyzer.rb:22:in `cached_tweets'
     # ./code/ruby/twits/lib/tweet_analyzer.rb:11:in `word_frequency'
     #
./code/ruby/twits/spec/revisions/tweet_analyzer4.13_spec_fail.rb:21:in
 `block (2 levels) in <top (required)>'

  3) TweetAnalyzer can find word frequency for a number of tweets
     Failure/Error: histogram = @analyzer.word_frequency(3)
     Mongo::ConnectionFailure:
       Failed to connect to a master node at localhost:27017
     # ./code/ruby/twits/lib/tweet_analyzer.rb:22:in `new'
     # ./code/ruby/twits/lib/tweet_analyzer.rb:22:in `cached_tweets'
     # ./code/ruby/twits/lib/tweet_analyzer.rb:11:in `word_frequency'
     #
./code/ruby/twits/spec/revisions/tweet_analyzer4.13_spec_fail.rb:27:in
 `block (2 levels) in <top (required)>'

Finished in 0.01098 seconds
4 examples, 3 failures
```

To fix this problem, we need to pull some of this connection mocking code out into a helper method in the spec:

```
ruby/twits/spec/tweet_analyzer_spec.rb
  def mock_collection
    Mongo::Connection.should_receive(:new).
      and_return(mock_connection = double("connection"))
    mock_connection.should_receive(:db).with("twitterCache").
      and_return(mock_db = double("db"))
    mock_db.should_receive(:collection).with("bill").
      and_return(mock_collection = double("collection"))
    mock_collection
  end
  it "caches tweets in Twitter to prevent multiple requests" do
    20.times { |i| @queried_tweets << "remote #{i}" }
    tweet_docs = (0..19).map {|i| {'tweet' => "cached #{i}"}}
    mock_collection.should_receive(:find).and_return tweet_docs

    histogram = @analyzer.word_frequency(40)
    histogram["remote"].should == 20
    histogram["cached"].should == 20
  end
end
```

Note that we changed the mock_collection variable into a method that returns the mock collection. This completely abstracts the rather gnarly connection and database setup that Mongo requires and allows the test to focus on describing the interaction with the collection.

Of course, merely pulling out this helper method does not fix our tests (which Autotest kindly brings to our attention). Note, however, that all of the tests are failing in the same way. All of the current failing tests now require something that they didn't require before—an empty cache of tweets.

The tests are telling us something. They're telling us that there's a context here that used to represent the only valid context for TweetAnalyzer but now is only one of two possible contexts. One way to describe that context would be to say that the TweetAnalyzer has no cached tweets. Let's create that context in the spec and move our failing examples into it:

```
ruby/twits/spec/tweet_analyzer_spec.rb
describe "with no cached tweets" do
  before( :each ) do
    mock_collection.should_receive(:find).and_return []
  end

  it "finds the frequency of words in a user's tweets" do
    @queried_tweets << "one"
    histogram = @analyzer.word_frequency(3)
```

```
    histogram["one"].should == 1
  end

  it "asks the users for recent tweets" do
    @queried_tweets << "one two" << "two"
    histogram = @analyzer.word_frequency()
    histogram["two"].should == 2
  end
  it "can find word frequency for a number of tweets" do
    @queried_tweets << "one" << "two two" << "three three three"
    histogram = @analyzer.word_frequency(3)
    histogram["one"] = 1
    histogram["two"] = 2
    histogram["three"] = 3
  end
end
```

Finally, Autotest tells us that we're done:

```
....

Finished in 0.01577 seconds

4 examples, 0 failures
```

4.5   Closing the Loop

Once we start running our code all the time, it becomes a lot easier to experiment with it. A key difference between interacting with code and merely editing code is that when we're interacting with code, we write code that we intend to delete. Usually when you're just editing code, you're trying to write code that you want to stick around and become part of your software. When we interact with code, we may wind up writing code that we have no intention of keeping. We may even wind up writing code that we know (or think) is wrong, just to prove that it is wrong or to see how it fails. As we saw in this chapter, a good portion of the database-related code we wrote wound up either being deleted or moved once the tests passed.

The idea here is that we're just adding code to gain information. Remember that productivity in software is not determined by lines of code but by value delivered to a customer. When writing this code, we're not creating the software, we're conducting experiments that give us insight and information about the problem we're trying to solve. Once we have the information, we may not need the code any longer. Whether it's the language, a third-party library, our development environment, our tools, or whatever else, we're just trying to discover something and learn more about what's going on.

Now what?

- Using inline assertions can help you probe the untested edges of your system to look for places where you're taking on more risk than is prudent. Try looking around and see how long it takes you to find untested conditions (even if the code is "covered").

- In this chapter, we mocked out database interactions by connecting to a real database first. You can use this approach with just about any third-party library that you may not know well enough to mock out by memory. For example, try exploring Ruby's filesystem API by manipulating files from tests and then selectively mocking out the parts that create inconsistency.

- Printing information to the Autotest window is one use of diagnostic methods. Can you think of others? What do you find yourself hunting for when writing code? Would integrating these methods with your editor or IDE provide additional value?

- For those familiar with REPL (Read-Evaluate-Print Loop) environments, the techniques in this chapter may seem very familiar. What are some effective techniques for REPL environments that could be translated to CT?

- In Section 4.2, *Comparing Execution Paths*, on page 58, we added comparison methods for type and behavior. Can you think of other ways to compare collected objects?

Part II — Rails, JavaScript, and Watchr

CHAPTER 5

Testing Rails Apps Continuously

In the first half of this book, we looked at how to create, extend, and use a continuous testing environment for a Ruby project. We saw how to run tests continuously to get feedback, and we also saw that tests are not the only way to quickly validate our work. Whether that work manifests itself as a business rule encoded in a method or as a default setting in a configuration file, all of this must be verified somehow, and there's no reason to wait to get that feedback.

In the second half of this book, we're going to create the same kind of environment for a Rails application. While the principles are the same, the tools and techniques we'll use are a little different. In a Rails project, we've got a lot more to worry about than just your typical Ruby code. We have database migrations that have to work properly (both up and down, thank you); configuration and environment files that must be correct; and style sheets, seed data, and probably a half-dozen other things that are specific to a particular project. And, of course, on top of all that we have our JavaScript code, which needs to be tested as well. We'll take a very close look at testing that JavaScript in Chapter 6, *Creating a JavaScript CT Environment*, on page 91, and in Chapter 7, *Writing Effective JavaScript Tests*, on page 103.

In this chapter, we're going to look at some ways to create rapid feedback loops for some of the parts and pieces that make up a typical Rails project. Beyond simply running specs continuously, we'll give you some examples of how to verify some of the changes you might make to a Rails project—from views to routes to migrations—thereby getting the same benefits of continuous testing no matter what parts of the system you're changing.

5.1 Building Our Rails App

There are lots of tools at our disposal for getting rapid feedback, especially when working in Rails. To demonstrate some of these tools, we'll create a Rails application called Groceries that (not surprisingly) generates grocery lists (Figure 4, *Grocery*, on page 81). We'll then work through some specific examples of how to create feedback loops for this kind of application. However, these examples are not intended to be exhaustive or even authoritative. The Rails community adopts new technologies quickly, and we hope these examples primarily serve to inspire you about how to create rapid feedback loops on your own projects with whatever tools you happen to be using.

To create our app, we'll need to run a few simple commands. First, we'll initialize our project, telling Rails to skip Test::Unit support:

```
$ rails new groceries --skip-test-unit
$ cd groceries
```

Then we'll add RSpec to our Gemfile:

```
ruby/groceries/Gemfile
group :development, :test do
  gem 'rspec-rails', '2.5.0'
end
```

Now we need to use Bundler to get RSpec and install it in our Rails app:

```
$ bundle
$ rails generate rspec:install
```

Next we'll create a couple of models and a scaffold to represent our grocery list:

```
$ rails generate model GroceryItem list_id:integer name:string quantity:string \
    bought:boolean
$ rails generate scaffold GroceryList name:string
$ rake db:migrate
$ rake db:test:prepare
```

And finally, we'll start up the server and make sure everything worked:

```
$ ./script/rails server
$ open http://localhost:3000/grocery_lists/new
```

5.2 Creating a CT Environment with Watchr

Autotest is a very effective tool for running tests. While it can be extended, there are many other tasks that we might want to do that aren't really related to tests. Watchr is a tool that allows us to easily perform arbitrary tasks in

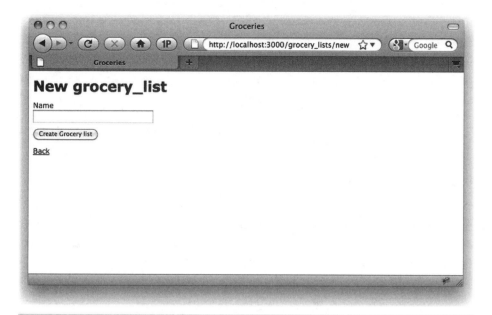

Figure 4—Grocery

response to file system changes. Unlike Autotest, it is not specifically designed to run tests (although it can be made to do that). It is, however, much more flexible than Autotest and can be easily configured to do other things. But first, we have to add it to our Gemfile:

```
$ gem install watchr
```

Now we can start Watchr by giving it a small snippet of Ruby code that describes what files we want to watch and what we want to happen when those files change:

```
$ watchr -e "watch('^app/(.*\.rb)')  { |m| puts %{You changed: #{m[1]}} }"
```

Here, by passing a regular expression to the watch() method, we're saying that we want Watchr to watch all .rb files under the app directory. watch() is defined by Watchr and is automatically available to any Watchr script we write.

In response to any change to those Ruby files, we'd like Watchr to print out the name of file. So we've also passed a block to the watch() method that takes the resulting match as a parameter. Note that because of the group we added to the regular expression, the match that contains the filename also has any matching directories under the app directory. Also note that since this script is pretty bare, Watchr will just look for changes when it starts without performing any other tasks.

If, however, we go ahead and change a file in our project (say application_controller.rb), then Watchr will report that it detected the change:

```
You changed: controllers/application_controller.rb
```

Awesome. Now let's look at some ways we can use this newfound power in a Rails project.

5.3 Validating Style Sheets

Testing views is a tricky thing. Whether it's in Rails or any other MVC framework, testing our presentation layer requires that we consider a lot of different factors, not the least of which is the fact that it's usually hard to tell if you got it right until you can see it on the screen.

Those special constraints don't mean, however, that we can't test our view code continuously. In fact, creating rapid feedback loops can be extremely helpful when working with code that isn't easily verifiable through automated means.

In our app, we're using a CSS3 extension named Sass.[1] Sass adds things like variables, mix-ins, and nested rules to CSS and plays very well with Rails. Another benefit of Sass is that we can quickly validate the syntax of a style sheet using the sass --check command. That means we can set up a Watchr rule to validate our style sheets continuously. But first we need to install Sass, which is part of the haml gem:

```
ruby/groceries/Gemfile
gem 'haml', '3.0.25'
```

To do this, we'll first create a rule in Watchr to watch for changes to .sass files. But rather than creating this rule on the command line, using the -e option, we can create a Ruby script and have Watchr use that to configure its rules instead. We'll go ahead and make a new file in our project called rails.watchr. Note that you can use whatever name you want for this script and that you can create different scripts for different environments or modes of working.

Once we've created a script file, we can add a rule watch for changes to .sass files and validate them:

---

1. http://sass-lang.com

```
ruby/groceries/rails.watchr
watch('^public/stylesheets/sass/(.*\.sass)') { |m| check_sass(m[1]) }

def check_sass(sass_file)
  system("clear; sass --check public/stylesheets/sass/#{sass_file}")
end
```

Now we're going to try out our new rule and introduce some new styling on a view. First we'll start Watchr with the script file:

```
$ watchr rails.watchr
```

Now we can make a change to one of our style sheets to make sure Watchr is paying attention. First, let's introduce an error:

```
ruby/groceries/public/stylesheets/sass/application.sass
div#toolbar
  background-color; black
```

Watchr detects the change to this file and then runs the command to validate the change, producing this message:

```
WARNING on line 3 of
code/ruby/groceries/public/stylesheets/sass/application.sass:
This selector doesn't have any properties and will not be rendered.
Syntax error: Invalid CSS after "background-color": expected
selector, was "; black"
        on line 3 of
code/ruby/groceries/public/stylesheets/sass/application.sass
  Use --trace for backtrace.
```

Replacing the semicolon with a proper colon will fix the problem. Doing so yields this:

```
   exists stylesheets/ic/stylesheets/sass
  compile public/stylesheets/sass/application.sass
overwrite stylesheets/ic/stylesheets/sass/application.css
```

Now, as we make changes to our style sheets, we'll know immediately if we make a syntax error. While this kind of syntax checking is common in most editors and IDEs for well-known formats like CSS, good support is harder to find with a newer format like Sass. By using Watchr to quickly create this feedback loop ourselves, we can get the same quick feedback you'd expect from an IDE, even when using a format that is too new to have good IDE support. This lets us take full advantage of newer technologies without having to wait for tool vendors to catch up with current trends.

5.4 Migrating Continuously

It can be really annoying to make changes to your database schema. Often times, developers shy away from refactoring their databases because of the cost of making minor changes (and the fear of making major ones). If you're not familiar with Rails migrations, these files define incremental changes to our schema. Any pending migrations can be applied, in order, to bring the schema up-to-date or roll it back to a previous state. Migrations make incremental database refactoring relatively cheap and easy and prevent us from having to define the "perfect" data model up front.

Of course, migrations aren't a free lunch. First, in order to check if the migrations are valid, you have to run them. Then, once they run, you have to run your tests to make sure the schema changes haven't broken anything (or, at least, haven't broken anything you didn't expect to break). However, this is a great opportunity for creating another feedback loop in our project, one that will help us make schema changes faster and let us explore different options when trying to design our database.

About Migrations

In Section 5.1, *Building Our Rails App*, on page 80, we created two simple models for our Rails app: GroceryList and GroceryItem. The generated scripts have created two migrations for us: db/migrate/20110301035911_create_grocery_lists.rb and db/migrate/20100820123037_create_recipes.rb. We can apply them now by running this command:

```
$ rake db:migrate
```

If it wasn't already, our schema should now be loaded into the development database (which is the default environment). We can verify this using the dbconsolecommand in Rails and querying for our schema:

```
$ ./script/rails dbconsole
sqlite> .schema

CREATE TABLE "grocery_items" ("id" INTEGER PRIMARY KEY AUTOINCREMENT
NOT NULL, "list_id" integer, "name" varchar(255), "quantity"
varchar(255), "bought" boolean, "created_at" datetime, "updated_at"
datetime);
CREATE TABLE "grocery_lists" ("id" INTEGER PRIMARY KEY AUTOINCREMENT
NOT NULL, "name" varchar(255), "author" varchar(255), "created_at"
datetime, "updated_at" datetime);
CREATE TABLE "schema_migrations" ("version" varchar(255) NOT NULL);
CREATE UNIQUE INDEX "unique_schema_migrations" ON "schema_migrations"
("version");
```

That looks about right. In addition to the default Rails columns like created_at, GroceryItem has a name, a quantity, and a reference to GroceryList, which just has a name.

Checking Migrations

When we created our models, we just gave them the barest of attributes, and now it's time to add some more. Looking at this schema, it seems we've missed something. GroceryList has a name, but it doesn't have any other information, like the creator's name. If we had already deployed this application, we would need to make another migration to transform our schema without destroying any existing GroceryList data. But since we're still in development, we can just modify the create_recipes migration.

Of course, as we make changes to these migrations, we want the same rapid feedback that we get by running our tests continuously. To do this, we're going to create a new rule in our Watchr script to watch for changes to migration files:

```
ruby/groceries/rails.watchr
watch('^db/migrate/(.*)\.rb') { |m| check_migration(m[1]) }
def check_migration migration_file
  system("clear; rake db:migrate:reset")
end
```

This will reapply all of our migrations to the test environment on each change. While this might seem like overkill, it runs fairly quickly, and it ensures that all of our migrations work when applied in order. Now we can add our attributes to GroceryList:

```
ruby/groceries/db/migrate/20110301035911_create_grocery_lists.rb
class CreateGroceryLists < ActiveRecord::Migration
  def self.up
    create_table :grocery_lists do |t|
      t.string :name
      t.string :author

      t.timestamps
    end
  end

  def self.down
    drop_table :grocery_lists
  end
end
```

As soon as we save the change, Watchr tells us that our migrations have run successfully.

```
==  CreateGroceryItems: migrating ================================================
-- create_table(:grocery_items)
   -> 0.0015s
==  CreateGroceryItems: migrated (0.0016s) ======================================

==  CreateGroceryLists: migrating ================================================
-- create_table(:grocery_lists)
   -> 0.0012s
==  CreateGroceryLists: migrated (0.0013s) ======================================
```

If we had introduced an error (like adding an extraneous comma after :name), we would have immediately gotten an error like this:

```
rake aborted!
./db/migrate/20110301035911_create_grocery_lists.rb:5: syntax error, unexpected \
  tSYMBEG, expecting kEND
      t.string :author
            ^
```

5.5 Running Rails Specs Fast

Back when we created our project, the Rails generators created some specs for us. We'd like to get those specs running continuously, but first let's try running our tests and make sure they pass:

```
$ rake
...............***............

Pending:
  GroceryListsHelper add some examples to (or delete) /Users/brady/\
    workspace/groceries/spec/helpers/grocery_lists_helper_spec.rb
    # Not Yet Implemented
    # ./spec/helpers/grocery_lists_helper_spec.rb:14
  GroceryItem add some examples to (or delete) /Users/brady/workspace/\
    groceries/spec/models/grocery_item_spec.rb
    # Not Yet Implemented
    # ./spec/models/grocery_item_spec.rb:4
  GroceryList add some examples to (or delete) /Users/brady/workspace/\
    groceries/spec/models/grocery_list_spec.rb
    # Not Yet Implemented
    # ./spec/models/grocery_list_spec.rb:4

Finished in 0.41526 seconds
30 examples, 0 failures, 3 pending
```

Hmm...they're passing (with a few pending tests), but that seemed to take a *really* long time to run. The actual tests were fast, less than half a second, but the setup time seemed really slow. Let's double-check that:

```
$ time rake
Finished in 0.64437 seconds
30 examples, 0 failures, 3 pending
```

```
real     0m11.831s
user     0m7.680s
sys      0m1.504s
```

11.8 seconds?!?! Oh, my goodness. That just won't do. We can't use this as our primary feedback loop if it takes eleven seconds to run thirty tests. We'll have to find a faster way to run these specs. Thankfully, we can use Watchr and the Spork gem we mentioned earlier (*Spork*, on page 39) to make things run faster. Spork keeps a "magazine" of forked processes running, each one preloaded with the Rails environment. When we need to run some tests, Spork chooses one, loads our application code, and runs our tests.

Optimizing this feedback loop is essential. Although we don't have a lot of tests right now, our test suite already takes over ten seconds to run. In our experience, if the tests take any longer than a second or two to run, we start looking for things to do while they're running—nothing kills productivity more than fighting the urge to check email or the Web after every save.

Faster Specs with Spork

We've already got Watchr installed, but we still need to get Spork:

ruby/groceries/Gemfile
```ruby
group :development, :test do
  gem 'rspec-rails', '2.5.0'
  gem 'spork', '0.8.4'
end
```

After adding Spork to our Gemfile and running bundle install, we're ready to set up Spork. We'll start that process by running the Spork bootstrap in the root directory of our Groceries app:

```
$ spork --bootstrap
```

This has added some code to the beginning of our spec_helper.rb file. We'll need to move all of the initialization code that was in our spec_helper into the prefork() block. This will tell Spork how to initialize the environment we'll use to run our tests. All of the time currently taken setting up this environment should then be eliminated when running tests after a file change. After moving that code, our spec_helper looks like this:

ruby/groceries/spec/spec_helper.rb
```ruby
require 'rubygems'
require 'spork'

Spork.prefork do
  # This file is copied to spec/ when you run 'rails generate rspec:install'
  ENV["RAILS_ENV"] ||= 'test'
```

```
require File.expand_path("../../config/environment", __FILE__)
require 'rspec/rails'

# Requires supporting ruby files with custom matchers and macros, etc,
# in spec/support/ and its subdirectories.
Dir[Rails.root.join("spec/support/**/*.rb")].each {|f| require f}

RSpec.configure do |config|
  config.mock_with :rspec
  config.fixture_path = "#{::Rails.root}/spec/fixtures"
  config.use_transactional_fixtures = true
end
end


Spork.each_run do
# This code will be run each time you run your specs.
end
```

Now we need to actually start the Spork server:

```
$ spork
```

And finally, we can test the speed of our test suite. Notice how we have to pass the –drb option to RSpec to tell it to use Spork:

```
$ time env rspec --drb spec
Finished in 0.4296 seconds
30 examples, 0 failures, 3 pending

real    0m0.971s
user    0m0.195s
sys     0m0.078s
```

There we go—that's *much* faster. It takes less than a second from start to finish, and it takes less than 300 ms of actual CPU time to load our application environment and run our tests. Now we've got a test suite that's fast enough to run all the time. Of course, we don't want to have to do all these steps manually, so now we're going to configure Watchr to do them for us.

Automating Spork with Watchr

To start out, let's add some watch() for RSpec specs:

This will watch for changes to .rb files under the app directory and to spec files under the spec directory, and then it will run the corresponding specs. The definition of "corresponding" here is pretty loose: any part of the spec's filename or path would match the spec. So a change to a file named user.rb would trigger both user_spec.rb and user_session_spec.rb to be run. As long as your specs are running quickly, this isn't a problem and can sometimes be pretty useful. But again, we can configure this however we like, so if it creates a problem we can quickly change it.

So if we restart Watchr and make a change to one of our specs (say, grocery_list_spec.rb), we get output that looks like this:

```
Finished in 0.00239 seconds
1 example, 0 failures, 1 pending
```

Perfect! Nice and fast, too.

Tracking Test State

So now we're running specs with Watchr, but it's only (generally) running one spec per change. One possible problem with this is that if another test starts to fail, you may not notice it until you run a full build. As we saw in Section 2.1, *Getting Started with Autotest*, on page 11, Autotest gets around this problem by rerunning all the tests after all of the known failing tests start to pass. While we don't need to rewrite Autotest in Watchr, it might be nice to run all the tests when a test passes, just to make sure we haven't missed anything. To do that, we're going to make some changes to our Watchr script:

```
ruby/groceries/rails.watchr
watch('^spec/spec_helper\.rb') { run_all_tests }
def run_all_tests
  @all_tests_passing = run(all_specs.join(' '))
  puts 'All tests pass' if @all_tests_passing
end

def run_test_matching(thing_to_match)
  matches = all_specs.grep(/#{thing_to_match}/i)
  if matches.any?
    @all_tests_passing &= run(matches.join(' '))
    run_all_tests unless @all_tests_passing
  end
end
```

The first thing we did here is introduce a little state into our Watchr script in the form of a variable named @all_tests_passing. We also added a watch() call to run all our tests if the spec_helper.rb changes. Finally, we added some methods to find and run all the specs in our suite and changed the run_test_matching() method to run all the tests after failure (that is, if run() returns a non-zero value).

This is a definite improvement over just running each corresponding test on every change. If we don't do this check, it's possible that while we're working to get one test to pass, we might cause another one to fail without realizing it. We want to make sure that if any of our tests fail, we're working on adding the necessary behavior to make them pass—and nothing else. Adding new behavior on top of something that's broken usually leads to waste.

Now that we've got our environment set up, we should be able to jump in and start building the rest of our app. Those pending tests are probably a good place to start. As we build out our application, our continuous testing environment will keep us on track by giving us feedback as quickly as possible. We'll be able to rely on our environment to tell us when something goes wrong, and that will give us the confidence to go faster. Of course, we'll still need to continue to look for opportunities to create rapid feedback loops. The flexibility of Watchr makes it easy to create these loops as soon as we discover them.

5.6   Closing the Loop

A typical Rails app is full of little tasks that have to be done all the time. From updating config files to restarting development servers, even with all the automation Rails gives you out of the box, there's still a lot of things that get in the way of just writing code that makes things work. The reason it's not all automated for you is that everyone's project is different. But that doesn't mean you can't (or shouldn't) do it yourself.

Now what?

- Try using Autotest with autotest-rails and Watchr. Does one work better for your app?

- As an alternative to Watchr, check out Guard.[2] Like Watchr, it provides a DSL for responding to filesystem changes, but it also supports a plugin system like Autotest. Plugins for common setups (like RSpec) are available as gems.

- Look at some of the Rails plugins you're using and think about how they are configured. What needs to be checked when that configuration changes. Can you automate it?

- If you haven't already, look into Factory Girl. It makes creating mocks in tests a breeze. Try converting a few tests to see what improvements you can make.

---

2.   https://github.com/guard/guard

CHAPTER 6

Creating a JavaScript CT Environment

Most Rails developers feel comfortable writing tests for their models, views, and controllers. As we saw in Chapter 5, *Testing Rails Apps Continuously*, on page 79, it's not only possible but extremely valuable to automate the testing of other parts of the system as well. However, it can sometimes be tempting to leave the JavaScript in your views out of this equation. You may tell yourself that errors in the UI might lead to layout problems or create small anomalies in the presentation of data, but it's nothing that a browser refresh won't fix, right?

As we expand our use of JavaScript beyond simple manipulations of HTML and start building more substantial web applications with Rails, we're finding that critical business logic is making its way into the browser. This means that errors in our JavaScript can lead to more serious problems: calculation errors, logical inconsistencies, even the corruption or loss of customer data. If we're adding business logic in the browser, we need to test that code as rigorously as we test our middle and back-end systems.

Of course, not only do we test our JavaScript automatically, we also test it continuously. This means that instead of spending hours and hours clicking around a browser, trying to figure out why our code doesn't work, we spend most of our time adding new features—and keeping our users happy. In this chapter, we're going to enhance the CT environment we created in the previous chapter to continuously test the JavaScript in our Rails Groceries application. We'll take a look at some of the tools we use to create CT environments for JavaScript and show you how to use them to create rapid feedback loops on your own projects.

6.1 Using Node.js

As we saw in Section 2.4, *Writing Fast Tests*, on page 23, we need our tests to be fast, so fast that we can run hundreds of them per second. It's important to note that this is the *elapsed time* between when we kick off a test run and when the results are reported to us. If our test runner spends 5 seconds initializing, 0.0001 seconds running tests, and 2 seconds processing results before reporting them, then we don't really have a fast test suite.

V8 is Google's open source JavaScript engine. It's used in Google's Chrome web browser and is really fast.[1] V8 is also the JavaScript engine used in *Node.js*, a JavaScript runtime environment suitable for server-side development. Node provides not only a wrapper around the V8 JavaScript engine but also fairly extensive libraries for writing event-driven applications purely in JavaScript. With a little bit of tweaking, we can run our tests in Node and have them run extremely fast so that we can get the continuous feedback we want without having to deal with running tests in a browser. But first we have to install it.

Node is distributed as a source tarball, so if you've never built a package from source using make, now's your chance. (It's easy, really.) We'll need to unpack the tarball and then build it like so:

```
$ wget http://nodejs.org/dist/node-v0.2.3.tar.gz
$ tar -xvf node-v0.2.3.tar.gz
$ cd node-v0.2.3
$ ./configure
$ make
$ make install
```

Now we can confirm that Node is installed properly by just running node:

```
$ node
> console.log("hello world");
hello world
```

Node is a very powerful environment to work in. We're going to be writing code that is designed to run in a web browser, but our tests will run in Node. That means that we can take advantage of all the features that Node has to offer when creating our test suite.

---

1. To find out how fast, try running Chrome's benchmarks for yourself at http://v8.googlecode.com/svn/data/benchmarks/v6/run.html.

6.2 Checking Syntax with JSLint

Developing cross-browser web applications is challenging enough. We don't need to make it any harder by queuing up a bunch of work. Tools like JSLint are essential weapons in the fight against the strange behavior found in legacy web browsers created by large software vendors from Washington state.

Most people don't think to run JSLint, however, until they have a problem. They run it and watch in horror as it reports hundreds of mistakes in their JavaScript code. Then they throw up their hands in despair and go back to debugging code with console.log(). We've certainly made this mistake before.

One option for preventing this problem is to integrate JSLint into a continuous integration build. That would certainly help, but if we're going to take the time to integrate this tool into our development environment, why not get feedback from it as fast as possible?

There is a Node.js package for JSLint that we can use to check the syntax of a JavaScript file. Using it is pretty easy, but, as of the time of this printing, installing it can be a little tricky. First, you need the Node package manager, npm. The lazy, trusting way to get it is by running the following:

```
$ curl http://npmjs.org/install.sh | sh
```

Note that you need to write permissions to the /usr/local/node directory in order to successfully run this script. More paranoid types should visit https://github.com/isaacs/npm and follow the instructions there. Installing npm as root is not recommended. Once you've installed npm, you can install the jslint package simply by running this:

```
$ npm install jslint
```

Now that the jslint package is installed, we can check one of the JavaScript files in our Rails project, like so:

```
$ jslint public/javascripts/shoppingList.js
OK
```

This seems to run pretty quickly, and, using the time utility, we can see exactly how fast it runs:

```
$ time jslint public/javascripts/shoppingList.js
OK

real    0m0.096s
user    0m0.063s
sys     0m0.021s
```

Not bad. Certainly fast enough to run on every change.

To integrate this into our CT environment, we're going to add a couple of Watchr rules:

ruby/groceries/rails.watchr
```
watch('^(public/javascripts/(.*)\.js)') do |m|
  jslint_check("#{m[1]}")
end

watch('^(spec/javascripts/(.*)\.js)') do |m|
  jslint_check("#{m[1]}")
end

def jslint_check(files_to_check)
  system('clear')
  puts "Checking #{files_to_check}"
  system("jslint #{files_to_check}")
end
```

Now whenever we change a JavaScript file, it will be automatically checked by JSLint, reporting any problems to us immediately after they occur (that is, after we create them). Forgetting a semicolon, for example, will yield an error like this:

```
Checking public/javascripts/shoppingList.js
  1 14,3: Missing semicolon.
    })
```

JSLint finds a lot of stuff that you would otherwise have to discover on your own. Running it from Watchr means we discover it right away, and that means we can stop relying on our browser to tell us if what we've written is even valid JavaScript. So now that we have some automated syntax checking in place, let's take a look at some tools for creating—and running—automated unit tests.

6.3 Writing FIREy Tests with Jasmine

There are a lot of options for writing unit tests in JavaScript, and we won't be able to cover them all here. However, since we're big fans of behavior driven development, we're going to take a look at our favorite BDD JavaScript framework, Jasmine.

Jasmine is a BDD framework written by Pivotal Labs[2] that takes a lot of inspiration from RSpec. It supports nested describe blocks, before and after setup methods, and comes with its own mocking framework.

---

2. http://pivotal.github.com/jasmine

In-browser Testing?

For the majority of tests, we prefer testing frameworks, like Jasmine, that don't have a DOM (document object model). Getting outside of the browser helps keep our tests fast and reliable. However, for some things, it makes sense to run tests in a browser. Anything that depends on browser-specific functionality, obviously, would need to be tested in a browser. And although it is possible to mock out the DOM API (using libraries like env.js and jsdom for example), it can also sometimes make sense to test DOM-dependent code in the browser itself.

Jasmine's mocking framework also includes a nice selection of matchers. You can also add your own matchers from a beforeXXX() method by calling this.addMatchers(). The mocking framework relies heavily on spies, rather than on pure mocks or stubs, and uses a syntax that works well with either classes or functions.

Since Jasmine is so similar to RSpec, we used it as our framework of choice for this book. We hope that you will find the techniques we demonstrate general enough to apply to whatever testing framework you like (or may already be using).

Creating a Spec Helper

Just like RSpec, Jasmine uses (by convention) a specHelper file to set up the necessary files to run our test. So if we want to start including JavaScript in our CT environment, the first thing we're going to need is a spec helper to support our Jasmine specs. This spec helper is going to need to do more than a typical RSpec spec helper, however, because we'll need to adapt the Node environment a bit to be able to test JavaScript that's destined for the browser. As a result, our spec helper looks like this:

```
ruby/groceries/spec/javascripts/specHelper.js
global.window = global;
global.navigator = {};

require('util/underscore');
require('util/modit');
require('util/moditTest');
require('application');
require('shoppingList');
require('funMenu');

_.extend(exports, global.app);
```

We're doing a few things here. First, we're defining a window variable in the global namespace. We're doing this because the global object in a browser environment can be accessed the window variable, while in Node the global variable is used. The first line in our spec helper unifies the discrepancy.

Next, we add a navigator variable. As with window, navigator is defined by the browser, and some of our code in this application depends on its existence.

Whenever we have a global variable like window or navigator that needs to be stubbed out on behalf of a lot of tests, we consider adding the stubs here in specHelper.js. In most cases, though, we add specific mocks and stubs to the tests that require them, using Jasmine's beforeEach() and beforeAll() methods to prepare them only when they are needed.

Now that we have our environment set up, we can invoke the require() calls that import the JavaScript files we have in our application. The parameters to these calls do not require a path or a file extension because Node is loading them from a predefined path (more on that later.) Node treats these required files as modules. Node has some specific rules about how modules are loaded, and we're taking advantage of them in our specHelper (which itself is a Node.js module).

The last line of the spec helper takes the global object, which has now been populated with the namespaces defined in the files that we required and copies the app namespace into the exports for this module. As we said, the spec helper is a proper Node.js module. Modules in Node have an exports variable that represents the module's public interface. The top level namespace for our applications is app, so by copying the contents of app into the module's exports, we effectively create a Node module that represents our entire application. As we'll see, this makes it possible to create a reliable test suite.

Writing a Test

So now that we have our specHelper configured, we can write a small Jasmine spec:

```
ruby/groceries/spec/javascripts/applicationSpec.js
describe('Groceries App', function() {
  var app;
  beforeEach(function() {
    app = require('specHelper');
  });

  it('loads on startup', function() {
    expect(app.start).toBeDefined();
  });
});
```

JavaScript Namespaces

JavaScript has no formal scoping mechanism. Unless otherwise specified, all objects coexist in a single global namespace. It (almost) goes without saying, but putting every object in your application into a single global namespace is a pretty bad idea.

To get around this, most developers define a global object that represents their entire application, and then they add children to that object to create individual namespaces that contain their functions and objects. This means that instead of just referencing a function like currentTime(), we must qualify it using the namespace like app.time.currentTime(). While this does mean some extra typing, it allows us to safely mix third-party libraries into our application without worrying about stomping all over someone else's functions and objects. It also ensures that we don't accidentally collide with our own names. As such, this practice has become commonplace in the JavaScript community.

And don't worry about the extra typing. In Section 1.6, *Introducing Modit*, on page 122, we'll show you a tool that can help eliminate it while retaining the benefits of a well-partitioned tree of namespaces.

Notice that in the beforeEach() method in this test, we required our specHelper Node.js module and assigned it to the app variable. As we mentioned in the last chapter, we're using app as the top level namespace for our application, so to keep a consistent name, we're using app as the name of the variable for the specHelper module. It's important to note, however, that app is not a global variable. We're explicitly loading our application into this variable from within our test.

If you've read *Behavior Driven Development*, on page 18, this structure should seem very familiar. Notice the call to require('specHelper') in the beforeEach() method. That is loading our specHelper module and assigning the resulting object to a variable defined inside the describe() block. We'll be able to access that variable in our tests. For now, we're just asserting that we can invoke a method and that it returns something. Our primary concern at this point isn't writing exhaustive tests, it's making sure that we have a fast, reliable, and informative environment to work in (we'll get to exhaustive in Chapter 7, *Writing Effective JavaScript Tests*, on page 103).

6.4   Running Tests Using Node.js and Watchr

Now that we have (what we think is) a failing test, we'll need to run it. Just as with JSLint, we want our Jasmine tests to run *fast*. So in this section, we're going to look at how to run some basic Jasmine tests using Node.js and Watchr. To get these tests running, we're going to use Misko Hevery's

Jasmine module[3] for Node.js, making just a few modifications to get it working with our Rails project. The first thing we'll need to do is add it to our application. The tricky part about this is that jasmine-node isn't a Rails plugin; it's designed to work with a Node project. So we're going to have to adapt it to our needs. Our first task is to decide where to put it.

For our project, we're going to check out this repo into vendor/js. This is not a standard location by any means, but hey, we're breaking new ground here. The next thing we're going to have to do is tweak a path in one of jasmine-node's files to get it to work with the Rails directory structure. We'll need to change the call to executeSpecsInFolder() in vendor/js/jasmine-node/specs.js to look like this:

`ruby/groceries/vendor/js/jasmine-node/specs.js`
```
jasmine.executeSpecsInFolder(__dirname + '/../../../spec/javascripts',
  function(runner, log){
    process.exit(runner.results().failedCount);
  }, isVerbose, showColors);
```

Now we're ready to run some tests.

Running Tests with Node.js

To get started, we need to make sure we can run our tests from the command line. The command for this is pretty unwieldy, so let's break it down:

```
$ env NODE_PATH=vendor/js/jasmine-node/lib:spec/javascripts:\
public/javascripts node vendor/js/jasmine-node/specs.js
```

As we mentioned in *Creating a Spec Helper*, on page 95, Node loads modules from a predefined path. We're defining that path here using the NODE_PATH environment variable. Node will scan this path for files that match the module name passed to a require() call (excluding the .js extension). Here, we're including the jasmine-node libraries, our specs, and our application's JavaScript files. Using that environment (defined by the call to env), we invoke the jasmine-node spec runner using node. The runner runs all of our tests, and it runs them very quickly.

```
$ time env NODE_PATH=vendor/js/jasmine-node/lib:spec/javascripts:\
public/javascripts node vendor/js/jasmine-node/specs.js
Started
F

groceries
  it has functions
  Error: Expected undefined to be defined.
```

---

3.   https://github.com/mhevery/jasmine-node

```
Finished in 0.01 seconds
1 test, 1 assertion, 1 failure

real    0m0.096s
user    0m0.063s
sys     0m0.021s
```

It's plenty fast, but it failed (that's actually a good thing—it's supposed to fail). To get this test to pass, we just need to add enough code to create the namespace and function (app.start()):

ruby/groceries/public/javascripts/application.js
```
modit('app', function() {
  function start() {}

  this.exports(start);
});
```

Since we haven't integrated this into our CT environment, we'll have to run that command again to see if the test passes:

```
$ env NODE_PATH=vendor/js/jasmine-node/lib:spec/javascripts:\
public/javascripts node vendor/js/jasmine-node/specs.js
Started
.

Finished in 0.012 seconds
1 tests, 1 assertions, 0 failures
```

Perfect. So now that we can run our tests, let's run them continuously.

Integrating Node and Watchr

To run our Jasmine tests continuously, we'll need to add the appropriate rules to Watchr. First, we'll need a method that runs the tests:

ruby/groceries/rails.watchr
```
def run_specs
  system('clear')
  load_path = "vendor/js/jasmine-node/lib:spec/javascripts:public/javascripts"
  system("env NODE_PATH=#{load_path} node vendor/js/jasmine-node/specs.js")
end
```

Notice how we've broken down the command we were running from the shell to make the parts a little more readable. The load_path variable specifies where Node.js should load our files from, and the system call placed at the very end of the method ensures that the return value of run_specs() will match the result of the test run (0 for passing, nonzero for failure). Now, we'll need to add the appropriate calls to watch():

ruby/groceries/rails.watchr
```
watch('^(public/javascripts/(.*)\.js)') { |m| run_specs }
watch('^(spec/javascripts/(.*)\.js)') { |m| run_specs }
```

Pretty straightforward, right? The problem is, this doesn't work. If we change a JavaScript file, the specs will run, but our JSLint checks won't. As of Watchr 0.6, rules defined later in the script take precedence over earlier rules. That means that if we want to both check our JavaScript files with JSLint and run tests using Jasmine, we're going to have to combine our two methods into one:

ruby/groceries/rails.watchr
```
watch('^(public/javascripts/(.*)\.js)') { |m| check_js("#{m[1]}") }
watch('^(spec/javascripts/(.*)\.js)') { |m| check_js("#{m[1]}") }

def check_js(file_to_check)
  run_specs if jslint_check(file_to_check)
end

def jslint_check(files_to_check)
  system('clear')
  puts "Checking #{files_to_check}"
  system("jslint #{files_to_check}")
end

def run_specs
  system('clear')
  load_path = "vendor/js/jasmine-node/lib:spec/javascripts:public/javascripts"
  system("env NODE_PATH=#{load_path} node vendor/js/jasmine-node/specs.js")
end
```

Now, whenever a .js file is changed, we check the syntax of the file using JSLint. If the syntax is OK (that is, the system() call returns a nonzero value), then we go ahead and run all the Jasmine specs in our project. We could probably filter the specs we run based on what file was changed, but they run so quickly that there's no reason to do that. This will give us a lot of feedback about our JavaScript very quickly and all with about ten minutes of work to configure it.

6.5 Closing the Loop

We find ourselves building fewer websites and building more single-page web applications (like Gmail, for example). The vast majority of the markup is generated on the fly, and an increasing amount of the business logic lives on the client. As browser technology gets better and better, we expect this trend to continue. As we move into this new environment, we're keen to bring with us the techniques that have worked so well on the server. In many ways, the interpreted nature of JavaScript makes this even easier.

Now we've set up an environment for continuously running tests against JavaScript. In the next chapter, we'll take a look at how to create an exhaustive JavaScript test suite, including some specific techniques for simulating a browser while running tests from Node. But first, check out some of the suggestions listed below. Ask yourself if it makes sense to integrate these tools and techniques into your projects.

Now what?

- Take a pass through the Node.js documentation. Remember that although your JavaScript may have to run in a web browser, your tests are running in Node. You can take full advantage of everything it has to offer in your tests.

- Perhaps you'd prefer good old RSpec to Jasmine? Check out the Ruby Racer,[4] a project that embeds the V8 JavaScript engine in Ruby.

- Do you already have in-browser tests? Try launching them using Watchr. Most browsers can be started from the command line with a URL given as a parameter. This can be a great way to run tests automatically when you need to run them in a browser.

- The jslint package for Node can't check more than one file at a time. When you have a few dozen JavaScript files, checking them all can start to get a little slow. Check out this fork on GitHub[5] for a version that lets you check more than one file at a time (it's pretty fast).

---

4.   https://github.com/cowboyd/therubyracer

5.   https://github.com/benrady/node-jslint

CHAPTER 7

Writing Effective JavaScript Tests

In the previous chapter, we focused mostly on creating a continuous testing environment for running JavaScript tests. We learned how to use a behavior driven development framework called Jasmine to create an informative test suite. We saw how running our tests in Node.js, rather than a browser, can make them fast and reliable. In this chapter, we're going to take a look at how to use the environment we created to make an exhaustive JavaScript test suite for the views in our groceries application.

In Section 6.4, *Running Tests Using Node.js and Watchr*, on page 97, we saw how Node.js can be used to run tests outside a browser. While we feel that in-browser testing of JavaScript UIs has its place, we prefer writing small and focused tests for our JavaScript, just like we do for our Ruby code. Running a lot of end-to-end tests or tests that depend on network resources such as servers and web services has always led us to slow, unreliable test suites. We've found an effective cure for this problem to be getting the tests out of the browser and running them in a much more controlled environment, like Node.js.

7.1 Mocking Out the Browser

Node.js is great and all, but when we use it to test code destined to run in a browser, we quickly encounter a pretty serious problem. There's no DOM (document object model) API. This means that our DOM-dependent code can't be readily tested, and any code that uses libraries that depend on the DOM (like JQuery) can't be tested either.

Thankfully, there is a W3C Level 2-compliant implementation of the DOM for Node.js named *jsdom*.[1] We can use it in our CT environment not only to

---

1.   https://github.com/tmpvar/jsdom

In-browser Record/Playback

Quite often, developers will try to write record- and playback-style tests that run in a web browser. There are a number of open source and commercial tools for this purpose, and we've seen a lot of teams that use them (with varying degrees of success). These kinds of tests exercise the application though the GUI, clicking on various UI widgets and scanning the resulting HTML for the result.

The problem with these sorts of tests is that while it is critically important to test our GUI widgets, conflating GUI testing with business logic testing always seems to result in tests that become unreliable. Coupling these two layers together means that a change to either one will cause tests to fail in both. This means that a single bug—or sometimes just an innocuous refactoring—can lead to dozens of confusing test failures that all must be rerecorded against the new code. If you're writing tests to be able to refactor without fear, these kinds of tests will not help you.

provide a DOM API but also to simulate a full browser environment, one that can be easily customized to help us write tests that are faster and more reliable.

Installing jsdom

We can install jsdom (and its dependency, htmlparser) using npm, the Node.js package manager. If you missed it, we described how to install npm in Section 6.2, *Checking Syntax with JSLint*, on page 93. The format of this command should feel very familiar to any Ruby programmer:

```
$ npm install htmlparser jsdom
```

As we saw before, Node.js modules can be loaded into a JavaScript variable using the require() function. We'll need to load jsdom in our specHelper.js so that we can use it to simulate a browser environment:

ruby/groceries/spec/javascripts/specHelper.js
```
var jsdom = require("jsdom");
```

We can use the functions on the jsdom object to create a mock browser environment for running tests. Now let's take a look at how to do that.

Creating a Window Object

In the previous chapter, we set up only the very basics of a browser-like environment by creating global window and navigator variables. Using jsdom, we can create a mock browser environment in our spec helper that is sufficient to support a DOM-dependent library like JQuery. Let's take a look at this setup in detail:

```
ruby/groceries/spec/javascripts/specHelper.js
window = jsdom.jsdom("<html><head></head><body></body></html>").createWindow();
global.navigator = {
  userAgent: 'jasmine'
};
global.window = window;
global.document = window.document;
global.location = "http://groceries.com";
```

First, using jsdom, we create a window that holds a very simple HTML document containing a head and a body. We then create a navigator object that defines a userAgent. We're adding this object as a child of the object stored in the global variable. We do this because variables that are defined in a Node.js module aren't automatically added to the global namespace the way they would be in a browser. To add something to the global namespace, Node.js provides this special variable, global, which we can add things to. In this case, we're using it to define variables that our browser-bound JavaScript expects to have. Finally, we set the window and document variables on the global object so they will be accessible outside this module.

If we have additional global properties that we want to remain constant across all of our tests, we would probably set them here on the global object. For example, JQuery 1.4.2 requires that the location variable be set, so we do that here. We can set any context-specific values from within the particular tests where they're needed.

Now we have a basic HTML document that we can use from within our tests. If we want to try to use JQuery, we must require it from our spec helper like so:

```
ruby/groceries/spec/javascripts/specHelper.js
require('util/jquery-1.4.2.js');
```

Now we'll assert that the body element exists:

```
ruby/groceries/spec/javascripts/applicationSpec.js
it('uses JQuery', function() {
  expect($('body').size()).toEqual(1);
});
```

A quick save and...

```
groceries
  It uses JQuery
  Error: ReferenceError: $ is not defined
```

Hmm...that doesn't seem to work. What's going on? The problem here is that JQuery isn't really a proper Node.js module. It adds its own properties (namely $ and jQuery) to the window variable. In a web browser, anything added to window is globally available, but this is not so in Node.js. We have to manually copy those variables into Node's explicit global variable like so:

ruby/groceries/spec/javascripts/specHelper.js
```
require('util/jquery-1.4.2.js');
if (window.$) {
  global.$ = window.$;
  global.jQuery = window.jQuery;
}
```

Another quick save...

```
Started
..

Finished in 0.01 seconds
2 tests, 2 assertions, 0 failures
```

and everything passes.

Cleaning Up the Document

At this point, we have a basic mock browser environment. One problem, though, is that it's all global. If we're not careful, we might develop some temporal dependencies between our tests and wind up with an unreliable test suite. What if we had a test that added some content to the document as part of its setup, for example, something that programmatically adds a title bar to the document when the app is started? Let's try writing a test for that:

ruby/groceries/spec/javascripts/applicationSpec.js
```
it('has a title bar', function() {
  app.start();
  expect($('#titlebar').size()).toEqual(1);
});
```

And we'll get this test to pass with a simple implementation for the start() function:

ruby/groceries/public/javascripts/application.js
```
modit('app', function() {
  function start() {
    $('body').append("<div id='titlebar'/>");
  }

  this.exports(start);
});
```

Now let's add another test for our title bar. Let's say we want to let the user toggle the visibility of the title bar with a click:

```
ruby/groceries/spec/javascripts/applicationSpec.js
it('User can hide the title bar by clicking on it', function() {
  app.start();

  // May be inconsistent because starting the app again created two title bars!
  $('#titlebar').click();

  expect($('#titlebar:visible').length).toEqual(0);
});
```

Depending on which test runs first, this will either pass or fail. Because the title bar is added on startup and we need to start the app to test the title bar, each test requires a clean environment in order to run reliably.

To combat this, we can re-create this environment after each test. But rather than adding that code to every single spec, we can give Jasmine a single function to run after each test using the beforeEach() function, just as we do in a spec's describe() function:

```
ruby/groceries/spec/javascripts/specHelper.js
beforeEach(function () {
  $('body').empty();
});
```

By placing this call right in the spec_helper.js file, we ensure that every test gets its own clean copy of our HTML document and that any modifications to that document do not affect any downstream tests.

7.2 Testing Asynchronous View Behavior

So now that we have a suitable continuous testing environment, let's use it to create a new view for our groceries application. This new view will display a generated shopping list and allow us to check off the items that we already have. We're going to do it purely in JavaScript, not only to serve as a better example but also because we are increasingly relying on JavaScript to dynamically build HTML, rather than mixing static HTML and JavaScript in our applications. As usual, we start with a test:

```
ruby/groceries/spec/javascripts/shoppingListSpec.js
describe('Shopping List', function() {
  var app;

  beforeEach(function() {
    app = require('specHelper');
  });
```

```
it('displays the items collected from the menu', function() {
  window.location = 'menus/6';
  var div = $('<div>');
  spyOn(jQuery, 'getJSON').andReturn([{}, {}]);

  app.view.shoppingList(div);

  expect(div.find('.shopping-list-item').length).toEqual(2);
  expect(jQuery.getJSON).wasCalled();
});
});
```

To make this test pass, we'll start by creating a JavaScript namespace called app.view and then defining a function in it named shoppingList():

```
ruby/groceries/public/javascripts/shoppingList.js
modit('app.view', function() {
  function shoppingList(div) {
    var list = $('<li>');
    var items = $.get('menus/6.json');
    _.each(items, function(item) {
      list.append($('<li>').addClass('shopping-list-item'));
    });
    div.append(list);
  }
  this.exports(shoppingList);
});
```

Reality Check

We'll stop here for a moment because a lot of the behavior of this widget is going to be determined by what information can be provided by our web app. The MenuController in our application sends back a summary of the menu, including a grocery list, when the requested format is JSON. In our test, we assumed that this was an array of objects (one object for each ingredient). To figure out the exact format of this response, we could walk through our model and controller code and try to assemble an example. Instead, we're going to manually query our Rails controller from our browser by entering the same URL we'll use later to query for the grocery list data. In our case, the query is http://localhost:3000/menus/6.json, and you can see the resulting JSON in Figure 5, *Fetching JSON*, on page 109.

Now that we have the format of the response we'll be getting from the server, we can go ahead and build our GUI control. Let's enhance our existing test by returning a snippet of our captured response as the result of jQuery.get():

Figure 5—Fetching JSON

ruby/groceries/spec/javascripts/shoppingListSpec.js

```
describe('Shopping List', function() {
  var response, app;

  beforeEach(function() {
    app = require('specHelper');
    response = {
      ingredients: [
        {
          needed: true,
          quantity: "1",
          unit: "loaf",
          name: "Sourdough Bread"
        },
        {
          needed: false,
          quantity: "2/3",
```

```
          unit: "cup",
          name: "milk"
        }
      ]
    };
  });

  it('displays the items collected from the menu', function() {
    window.location = 'menus/6';
    var div = $('<div>');
    spyOn(jQuery, 'getJSON').andReturn(response);

    app.view.shoppingList(div);

    items = div.find('.shopping-list-item');
    expect(items.length).toEqual(2);
    expect(items.first().text()).toEqual('1 loaf Sourdough Bread');
    expect(jQuery.getJSON).wasCalledWith('menus/6.json');
  });
});
```

And a quick save tells us if we're still passing:

```
Started
.....F

Shopping List
  It displays the items collected from the menu.
  Error: Expected 1 to equal 2.
```

Hmm...it seems the format of the response wasn't quite what we expected. Instead of a simple array of ingredients, our app returns an object that has a list of ingredients as a property. Good thing we caught that now. We'll go ahead and make the changes to our shoppingList() method and enhance the expectations to test the content of the list:

ruby/groceries/public/javascripts/shoppingList.js
```
modit('app.view', function() {
  function shoppingList(div) {
    var list = $('<ul>');
    var menu = $.getJSON('menus/6.json');
    _.each(menu.ingredients, function(item) {
      list
        .append($('<li>')
          .append($('<div>')
            .addClass('shopping-list-item')
            .text(item.quantity + " " + item.unit + " " + item.name)
          )
        );
    });
    div.append(list);
```

```
      }
      this.exports(shoppingList);
});
```

And a quick save tells us that we passed:

```
Started
......

Finished in 0.013 seconds
3 tests, 7 assertions, 0 failures
```

View Integration

At this point, we have a function that will build our shopping list widget, but we don't really have a good way to integrate it into our Rails view. To accomplish this, we're going to query for a particular div in our app's start() function and invoke our shoppingList() function on it:

ruby/groceries/public/javascripts/application.js
```
modit('app', function() {
  function createToolbar() {
    $('body')
      .append($("<div id='titlebar'/>")
        .click(function() {
          $(this).toggle();
        })
      );
  }

  function start() {
    createToolbar();
    $('#shopping-list').each(function(i, element) {
      app.view.shoppingList(element);
    });
  }

  this.exports(start);
});


$(window.document).ready(app.start);
```

Of course, we made a test for this code as well:

ruby/groceries/spec/javascripts/applicationSpec.js
```
it('creates the shopping list on startup', function() {
  spyOn(app.view, 'shoppingList').andReturn();
  $('body').append($("<div>").attr('id', 'shopping-list'));

  app.start();

  expect(app.view.shoppingList).wasCalled();
});
```

Degrading Browsers

It is important to note that this technique does not necessarily degrade gracefully to older browsers or to those that have JavaScript turned off. Whether or not this is appropriate for your project depends on, well, your project. In this case, our customers have modern browsers with JavaScript turned on, so we're not worried about degrading gracefully.

However, if you're building a large, consumer-facing application that needs to support a wide array of browser types, you may want to consider creating a traditional Rails view first. Using JQuery, you could then augment the markup to apply changes asynchronously to give users with modern web browsers a better experience while still supporting customers using older browsers.

Now all we need to do is add a simple div to our view to act as a placeholder for the shopping list:

```
<div id="grocery-list"/>
```

And that's it. If we needed to pass any additional information down to the client, we could do it here by adding attributes or elements to this div. As it stands, this is all we need.

7.3 Testing View Aesthetics

The appearance of UI elements in our views, created with HTML, CSS, and JavaScript, can be kind of tricky to test. As we saw in Section 7.2, *Testing Asynchronous View Behavior*, on page 107, it's entirely possible to check that our views generate the correct markup, but that does not guarantee that our interface actually looks good. User experience and user interface design is important—very important. Most users will judge the quality of your app by what they see, and what they see the most is your UI. Unfortunately, there is no testing framework on earth that has yet implemented the should-BePretty() matcher. Quite often, you just have to see it for yourself to know exactly how an HTML element will be rendered or whether a particular CSS style gives you the effect you want.

In this section, we're going to discuss a few techniques we've used to create rapid feedback loops when designing user interfaces. While we can't get automatic verification of beauty, we want fast feedback to help guide us in the direction we want to go, just as with other parts of our system. When creating these loops for UI work, they sometimes manifest themselves differently than in other parts of the system.

User Experience and Automated Testing

It almost goes without saying in the Ruby community, but we're going to say it anyway: you need to have a fast feedback cycle when working with user interfaces. The time between when you make a change that affects the appearance of your app and when you can see the results in a browser should only be a couple of seconds at most—essentially, however long it takes to refresh the browser. If we're working with a deployment environment that can't refresh this quickly (JRuby on J2EE, for example), we always take the time to either tweak the container to reload files on each request, or we find a way to deploy to a different environment for development (Thin or Webrick, for example). Wasting time in a lengthy build/restart loop when you're working with user interfaces is just silly. Take the time to make sure you can do it quickly and the investment will pay dividends quickly.

Finally, although it quite often makes sense to experiment with UI changes in the browser, we still want to write tests for the code that we create. At this point, the primary function of the tests is to serve as an informative record of why things are the way they are. This is especially true when adding the strange-looking hacks and workarounds that are sometimes necessary when dealing with a multibrowser user base. Rather than explaining this code with a comment, we prefer writing tests that demonstrate the exact context and behavior that each browser expects. Not only does this make refactoring easier, but it also makes it much more likely that when those quirks are corrected in later browser versions, we'll be able to recognize when workaround code can be eliminated.

Creating Test Harnesses

Creating a temporary test harness to test out a particular scenario in our UI can sometimes make a lot of sense. Instead of clicking through the application over and over again to re-create a particular state in the UI, we can just mock out the portions of the system that control that state. That way, visualizing our changes is as easy as refreshing the browser.

We usually create simple tests harnesses, toss them in the public directory, and delete them when we're done. They aren't designed to be reusable. On occasion, we've found ourselves slipping a bit and testing behavior (rather than appearance) using a test harness. We'll then pull some of the code from the harness into our test suite. But usually, test harness code doesn't last the day. That's because while the goal when creating them is increased understanding, test harnesses, due to their manual nature, aren't really informative or reliable (or fast, for that matter). Once we've achieved that understanding (that is, what markup we need to create the appearance we want), we want to encode it in our test suite where it will last.

Another guideline that we like to use when creating UI elements is to try to limit the number of branches in the logic of the code that creates the initial layout. A formal definition of this would be that we try to maintain a cyclomatic complexity of 1 for functions that create markup. This helps ensure that if the basic markup looks correct, it probably is correct. Of course, we can still test the structure of this markup using Jasmine if we have any doubts, but keeping branches out of the code helps limit the number of potentially different visual representations that we have to verify manually.

Fast Feedback Using the JavaScript Console

If you're not familiar with the Firefox plugin Firebug or Google Chrome's JavaScript console, you need to get acquainted very soon. These are indispensable tools for building web applications. They provide not only a JavaScript debugger and interactive console but also tools for inspecting and manipulating HTML.

At the most basic level, we can use these tools as a REPL[2] to experiment with snippets of JavaScript. Usually we use our CT environment for that, but there are some situations where using the browser console can be more convenient (when we don't have our CT environment running, for example).

However, the console that these tools provide is much more powerful than a plain JavaScript shell. It has complete access to not only the DOM of the currently loaded page but also all the publicly accessible JavaScript functions on that page. That means we can manipulate the HTML and CSS of the page ourselves in real time. It also means that we can invoke functions in our JavaScript code and immediately view the effects on the DOM. This makes it very easy to experiment with different formats and styles, letting us tweak our CSS and markup until it looks just right.

Like our test harnesses, however, these tools can only help us understand what our markup will look like when rendered by the browser. They can't encode that understanding in an informative way like a test can. So we want to be sure to create tests and/or modify existing tests whenever we decide on a particular presentation. That way, we don't have run through the app after making a change to make sure that everything looks OK.

---

2. Read-Evaluate-Print Loop—most interpreted languages (including JavaScript) have interactive consoles that let you execute one statement at a time.

7.4 Closing the Loop

JavaScript provides opportunities for a number of different feedback loops. Perhaps its most powerful feature is its ubiquity—by being available in the vast majority of web browsers around the world, JavaScript has secured its legacy with a giant developer community. This community has created a wide array of tools that help us create the rapid feedback loops we want.

Now what?

- The easiest test to write is no test at all. Instead of creating (and testing) your own custom UI widgets, try using a UI library like YUI (http://developer. yahoo.com/yui), Scriptaculous (http://script.aculo.us/), MooTools (http://mootools. net/), or Google's Closure (http://code.google.com/closure/).

- js-test-driver (http://code.google.com/p/js-test-driver/) is a project that aims to integrate browser and command-line environments. If using Node.js to run tests doesn't work for your project, this just might!

- We populated our grocery list with an asynchronous query, but how do we update it? Try using the jQuery.post() to publish data to a Rails controller using JavaScript. How can you quickly verify what the request should look like?

Part III — Appendices

Making the Case for Functional JavaScript

When working with JavaScript in a Rails application, it's easy to fall into the pattern of treating everything as a classical object. While writing Ruby, we get used to the idea of instantiating objects, invoking methods on them, and then passing the result of those invocations onto other objects. It's tempting to just follow this same pattern when we switch over to JavaScript.

However, we haven't had a lot of success simply translating the testing strategies and design techniques of the object-oriented world into JavaScript. The browser is a different environment, full of events, callbacks, and the ever-present DOM. Despite what you may have been led to believe, the language itself is different too. We suspect that others have run into the same problems, been discouraged by the results, and given up.

In this appendix, we'd like to introduce you to another way of writing JavaScript, one that we've come to like very much. It isn't as much about testing as it is about good design. But we thought that some of our readers who have struggled when trying to test JavaScript may, like us, simply be falling into a trap of poor design. A different approach was all we needed to make writing tests in JavaScript fluid and easy. We'll talk about how we structure and organize our JavaScript functions, discuss some alternatives to classical type hierarchies, and show you how to use one of our favorite JavaScript libraries, Underscore.js.

A1.1 Is JavaScript Object Oriented or Functional?

If the classical object-oriented approach doesn't produce the results we want, what are our alternatives? We think the language is actually quite suited to a more functional style of programming and that the design benefits of this style can be significant. In most cases, we can achieve these benefits simply by giving up a few of JavaScript's more dubious "features." So let's talk briefly about why JavaScript is the way it is and examine some techniques for creating highly testable JavaScript using a functional, rather than an object-oriented, style.

The Legend of JavaScript

JavaScript was renamed in December 1995 to help promote it as an alternative to Java applets. Before that, it was called LiveScript, and its creator, Brendan Eich, had been recruited to work at Netscape with the promise of "doing Scheme" in the browser.[1] Netscape was attempting to create a lightweight scripting language to complement the Java applet support it was adding to its upcoming browser release. In addition to the name, JavaScript intentionally uses some of the keywords and conventions found in Java (and other object-oriented languages). It even had a type system that allowed for reuse through inheritance, sort of like Java.

While these similarities were rather superficial, many developers familiar with Java (including us) treated JavaScript as a watered-down version of Java, using the same techniques in what was really a very different language and environment. In retrospect, this was a horrible idea. Douglas Crockford, the JavaScript architect at Yahoo who developed the JSON data format, laments, "I now see my early attempts to support the classical model in JavaScript as a mistake."[2]

This problem is exacerbated by the enormous amount of poorly written JavaScript that permeates the Internet. Aside from the myriad of horrible "examples" on blogs and technology websites, there is the Web itself. Since JavaScript is interpreted by the browser, it is quite easy to "borrow" JavaScript source code from another website and use it on your own. You don't even have to unobfuscate it first if you don't want to! After all, if IBM did it that way, it must be right. Right?[3]

So if we want our JavaScript tests to be reliable and informative while still keeping the code clean, we need to be very careful about how we design our system. We can't rely on the language features of JavaScript to lead us in the right direction. We're going to have to use it differently.

---

1. http://weblogs.mozillazine.org/roadmap/archives/2008/04/popularity.html

2. http://www.crockford.com/javascript/inheritance.html

3. For more about JavaScript's sordid past, see "JavaScript: The World's Most Misunderstood Programming Language," http://www.crockford.com/javascript/javascript.html.

Comparing Java and JavaScript

Java is an object-oriented language. JavaScript, on the other hand, has as much in common with functional programming languages like Scheme as it does with its namesake. It has objects and functions but no true classes. The inheritance model is prototype-based rather than class-based. Unless special measures are taken, all the variables on a JavaScript object are publicly accessible. There is no formal scoping mechanism for these objects, and unless otherwise encapsulated, they coexist in a single global namespace. Many JavaScript applications are made up of a set of these objects, and dependencies between them are uncontrolled and poorly defined.

This creates a serious problem when trying to test these applications. We find that designing for testability with a set of global objects often leads us away from good design rather than toward it. For example, this JavaScript "class" is testable:

```
ruby/groceries/public/javascripts/ooMenu.js
MenuController = function(items) {

  this.listenTo = function(div) {
    div.onclick(function(e) {
      items.push(e.element.text());
    });
  };
};
```

But, there's a lot of unnecessary code in there. Not only that, but take a look at what the test for this class looks like:

```
ruby/groceries/spec/javascripts/ooMenuSpec.js
describe('MenuController', function() {
  it('records which items have been clicked', function() {
    mockDiv = {};
    mockEvent = {
      element: {
        text: function() { return 'textValue'; }
      }
    };
    mockDiv.onclick = function() { };
    spyOn(mockDiv, 'onclick');
    var items = [];

    var controller = new MenuController(items);
    controller.listenTo(mockDiv);
    mockDiv.onclick.argsForCall[0][0](mockEvent);
    expect(items[0]).toBe('textValue');
  });
});
```

Yikes. To test the onclick() handler, we have to pass in a spy as the div, get the function passed to onclick() from the spy, invoke it, and then verify the results. When we write tests like this, we know there's a problem.

Using Functions in Namespaces

Instead of a set of objects, we prefer to build web applications in JavaScript from a hierarchy of namespaces that contain functions. We define these functions within the scope of a JavaScript module, which can contain any privileged functions that we may not want to make public. Functions depend only on functions in other namespaces. While it is possible to store state in a module and share that state across functions in the module, we tend to avoid that because it makes the functions more coupled and harder to test.

A1.2 Introducing Modit

As we discussed in Section 7.2, *Testing Asynchronous View Behavior*, on page 107, the module pattern detailed by Douglas Crockford in his book *JavaScript, The Good Parts* [Cro08], is a powerful one. It allows us to encapsulate functionality in a predictable way and avoid some of the more esoteric problems with JavaScript scoping, binding, and inheritance rules. We love this pattern and use it often. However, it does have its shortcomings. First, it takes a fair amount of boilerplate code to create a module, so it's tempting to create larger modules rather than smaller ones. But smaller modules encourage decoupling (and therefore, testability). So we wind up having to fight against the structure of the code to make things decoupled.

Another problem we've had with traditional JavaScript modules is that their dependencies must be fully qualified. As we saw in *JavaScript Namespaces*, on page 97, functions that use functions in other modules must include the entire name of the namespace, like app.time.formatters.short(). This creates duplication, makes mocking more difficult, and unnecessarily adds to the amount of code we have to type.

To help address these problems, we created a small (but mighty!) JavaScript module framework called *Modit*.[4] Modit is an open source framework that makes creating JavaScript modules easy. It automatically creates JavaScript namespaces and lets you define functions in them. Unlike traditional JavaScript modules, multiple Modit modules can live in the same namespace because Modit merges them automatically. Modit also provides other tools to cut down on clutter and boilerplate, such as aliases for dependent

---

4. https://github.com/benrady/modit

namespaces and functions. We also use Modit because it encourages us to create lots of small, decoupled modules rather than a just few big, complex ones. In other words, Modit is JavaScript modules with superpowers.

Superpower #1: Less Code

Let's compare traditional JavaScript modules to ones created with Modit. This module uses the traditional pattern:

```
ruby/groceries/public/javascripts/moditExample.js
if (app === undefined) { app = {}; }
if (app.example === undefined) { app.example = {}; }

app.example.mynamespace = (function() {
  function internalFunction() {
    return "internal";
  }

  function exportedFunction() {
    return "exported";
  }

  var exports = {
    exportedFunction: exportedFunction
  };
  return exports;
})();
```

For every module we make like this, we have to check to see if the namespace hierarchy exists and create it if necessary. Then we can define a function for our module, being sure to wrap it in parentheses and invoke it to create the namespace object. We have to create and return that namespace object, and for each of the functions we want to include, we have to give it an external name and a reference to the internal function name. That's a lot of code to type, and if we want to compose our system of lots of little modules, this can get tedious quickly. Compare that to this module, which provides the same behavior but was created with Modit:

```
ruby/groceries/public/javascripts/moditExample.js
modit('app.example.mynamespace', function() {
  function internalFunction() {
    return "internal";
  }

  function exportedFunction() {
    return "exported";
  }
  this.exports(exportedFunction);
});
```

Here, we rely on Modit to create the namespace hierarchy for us, if necessary. We then give Modit a function that defines our module and call this.exports to pick which functions we want to export into the namespace. Note that we don't have to define the external name of the function; it simply reuses the internal name.

Superpower #2: Explicit Dependencies

Modit lets you declare the namespaces you depend on explicitly. The most obvious benefit of this is eliminating duplication. Let's look at a JavaScript module written without explicit imports:

```
ruby/groceries/public/javascripts/imports.js
modit('app.example.view', function() {
  function updatedAt(recipes) {
    return "Last updated at " + app.example.time.format(recipe.updateTime,
      app.example.time.SHORT);
  }
  this.exports(updatedAt);
});
```

There's a fair bit of duplication here, and this code is a bit hard to read. Let's compare that to a module with explicit imports, created using Modit:

```
ruby/groceries/public/javascripts/imports.js
modit('app.example.view', ['app.example.time'], function(time) {
  function updatedAt(recipe) {
    return "Last updated at " + time.format(recipe.updateTime, time.SHORT);
  }
  this.exports(updatedAt);
});
```

By declaring the imports explicitly, we not only make these dependencies readily apparent, but we also remove duplication by providing a short-form reference to the namespace. This short form is declared as a function parameter rather than a local variable, which has other benefits.

One of the main benefits of this short form is that it prevents a particular kind of mistake that commonly makes tests unreliable. JavaScript doesn't give you a lot of constructs in the language to prevent mistakes. In some cases, it almost works against you. For example, it's very easy to unintentionally create global variables by simply forgetting to add a var keyword in front of a local variable. Those kinds of problems can wreak havoc on your test suite, causing it to pass one minute and fail the next, depending on what order your tests are run in. But declaring our imports as function parameters rather than variables means we can never forget the var keyword, which helps make our tests more reliable.

Superpower #3: Conditional Exports

Just like traditional JavaScript modules, the exports in Modit are explicit. Unlike traditional JavaScript modules, however, Modit handles merging the exported functions into the namespace. The call to this.exports() makes the given methods available in the namespace with a minimum of boilerplate code. This function may be called any number of times from anywhere in the module definition function.

The other benefit of defining exports this way is that we can export things conditionally. If we detect a particular type of browser or a third-party library like jQuery, we can optionally export functions or change which function is exported. This can be useful in a number of different situations.

Let's say we need our application to degrade gracefully across different browsers. For example, in newer browsers that support HTML5 local storage, we want to use that storage for saving user settings. Alternatively, in older browsers, we might want to fall back to using cookies. So we create a namespace for storage (app.storage), and in that namespace we define a function, such as saveCookie(). We can use this method to save data as a cookie no matter what kind of browser we're running on. But we can also conditionally define a saveLocal() function that is only available if HTML5 local storage is supported:

```
ruby/groceries/public/javascripts/conditional.js
modit('app.storage', function() {
  function saveCookie(item) {
    //save item to a cookie
    //...
  }

  function saveLocal(item) {
    // save item to HTML5 local storage
    //...
  }
  this.exports(saveCookie);

  if (typeof(localStorage) !== 'undefined' ) {
    this.exports(saveLocal);
  }
});
```

Now a use of that namespace can either depend on cookies for storage using the saveCookie() function or gracefully degrade from local storage to cookies if preferred, like so:

```
ruby/groceries/public/javascripts/conditional.js
modit('app', ['app.storage'], function(storage) {
  function saveItems(items) {
    _.each(items, storage.saveLocal || storage.saveCookie);
  }
});
```

By treating these functions as objects and using the || operator to pass one or the other as a parameter to each, we can remove duplication while still selectively supporting both methods of storage.

Superpower #4: Multimodule Namespaces

As we've seen, using the traditional module pattern gives you one module per namespace. With Modit, you can define multiple modules all within the same namespace and give each one its own closure. For example, let's say we wanted some functions in the app.storage namespace that would let us save key-value pairs. We could add these functions to our module that defines the other storage functions for HTML5 local storage, but then the internal data structure for the new functions would be exposed to the existing functions. To keep them separate, we can add those functions to that namespace in a different module, like so:

```
ruby/groceries/public/javascripts/storage.js
modit('app.storage', function() {
  var keystore = {};
  function saveValue(key, value) {
    keystore[key] = value;
  }

  function getValue(key) {
    return keystore[key];
  }

  this.exports(saveValue, getValue);
});
```

Simply by declaring this module in the same namespace as our other module, Modit will merge the functions from both into the namespace automatically. In addition, the closure created by the two module functions is kept separate, so that variables (like our keystore variable) are only accessible from within the module that defines them. This has a number of benefits, not the least of which is to make our tests more reliable by reducing the likelihood of a temporal dependency caused by state shared between functions.

Modit is one of the JavaScript libraries that we use when trying to build more functional JavaScript. In the next section, we're going to take a look at how to use Modit (and another library named Underscore.js) to take advantage of some of JavaScript's better language features. And while each of these techniques and libraries can be used independently, we think you'll find that if you put them all together, you'll wind up with something greater than the sum of their parts.

A1.3 Functional Programming in JavaScript

Now we're going to look at JavaScript a little differently. Rather than treating it as a pseudoclassical object-oriented language, we're going to try to make it more powerful by using fewer language features. We hope to make our tests (and the rest of our code) more informative by adopting a structure that communicates intent while providing for decoupling and reuse.

Using Underscore.js

Underscore.js[5] is an open source JavaScript library that provides lots of very useful functions. We have come to depend more and more on it as we have made our code more functional. One of the particularly powerful benefits that Underscore offers is the ability to work with higher order functions. For example, compose(), invoke(), and wrap() are all higher order functions that operate on functions. We can use these to assemble very sophisticated combinations of behavior with very little code and lots of testability.

Underscore gives us enormous power and flexibility when working with JavaScript's two primary data types: objects and arrays. One simple example of this would be flatten(), which takes composed arrays of arrays and flattens them into a single array:

```
> _.flatten([1, [2, 3], [[[4]]]])
[1, 2, 3, 4]
```

As you can see, Underscore gets its name from the fact that it defines a global variable _, which is used to invoke the functions in the library. flatten() is particularly useful when consuming the output of other functions that use arrays as intermediate structures. For example, if we combine two other functions in the Underscore arsenal, map() and values(), we could easily pick the values out of an array of objects:

```
> var namesArray = [{name1:'bill', name2: 'steve'}, {name1:'bob'}];
> var names = _.map(array, _.values);
> names
[ Array[2], Array[1] ]
```

---

5. http://documentcloud.github.com/underscore/

Higher Order Functions

In most object-oriented languages, like Ruby, behavior is attached to objects. Methods in Ruby are not objects themselves. They cannot, for example, be passed as parameters to other methods. Of course, other language constructs in Ruby, like blocks and procs, fill this void, but the majority of methods that we write are attached (either implicitly or explicitly) to another object.

In JavaScript, functions are objects unto themselves. That means you can create *higher order functions*, that is, functions that take other functions as parameters or that return functions as a result (or both). One common application of this is the _.compose() function in Underscore. This function takes a list of functions and returns a new function that chains the given functions together, passing the result of the first as a parameter to the next. Higher order functions are a very powerful feature of JavaScript—arguably its most powerful feature—and it is one of the things that makes Underscore so useful.

The map() function iterates through a collection (an array, an object, or another iterable value), passing each element to the iterator, which is the function provided in the second parameter. If the example above looks a little strange to you, remember that JavaScript has first-order functions, so we can pass them around like any other value. In this case, because we want the values on the object, we can use the Underscore function values() as the second parameter. We do this by leaving off the parentheses so that the function itself is passed, rather than it being invoked and having the return value passed. The only thing left to do is flatten the composed arrays and sort it:

```
> _.flatten(names).sort()
["bill", "bob", "steve"]
```

Of course, because we have higher order functions in JavaScript, we can write functions that operate on functions. One such function in Underscore is compose(), which takes a set of functions and composes them together, returning a new function that passes the result of each function to the next as a parameter. So if we wanted to create a function that would ensure that we don't get any duplicate names from the objects in our namesArray, we could create one programmatically by composing values() with the Underscore function for removing duplicate values from an array, uniq().

```
> namesArray = [{name1:'bill', name2: 'steve'}, {name1:'bob', name2: 'bob'}];
> var uniqValues = _.compose(_.uniq, _.values);
> _.flatten(_.map(namesArray, uniqValues));
["bill", "steve", "bob"]
```

The power of these kinds of functions alone might be enough to convince you to shy away from classical types and store your data in simpler composed structures. It certainly was for us. Now that we've given you a brief introduction to Underscore, let's take a look at some of the ways you can put it to good use.

Information Hiding through Functions

So if we're passing things around as one big object (as we usually are when, for example, processing a JSON response), how do we avoid becoming overly dependent on the structure of that object? Won't we have to change a lot of code to, say, introduce another kind of data into these objects? Furthermore, aren't we going to wind up with huge, unwieldy objects (maps of maps of arrays of maps of strings to arrays of...)? Yes, and no.

While the objects we pass around may be large, the manner in which we process them need not be. For example, let's assume that we had a controller in our Rails app that returned all the information for a particular user as a JSON document. That document might look something like this:

```
ruby/groceries/spec/javascripts/userSpec.js
response = {
  first_name: 'Bob',
  last_name: 'Dobilina',
  user_name: 'bdob',
  address: {
    street: '123 Fake St.',
    street2: '',
    city: 'Chicago',
    state: 'IL',
    zip: '60613'
  },
  phone_numbers: [
    { home: '773-555-2827' },
    { work: '773-555-2827' },
    { mobile1: '312-555-1212'},
    { mobile2: '773-555-1234'}
  ]
};
```

This is a fairly complex response object. It contains all the data we want, but some of it is nested two or three levels deep. How do we balance easy access to this data with ensuring that we isolate the effects of changing its structure?

The simplest approach would be to just pick out the data from this object ourselves wherever we need it, like so:

```
ruby/groceries/spec/javascripts/userSpec.js
it('has a first and last name', function() {
  expect(response.first_name + ' ' + response.last_name).toEqual('Bob Dobilina');
});
```

The problem with this is that it leaves our client code highly coupled to the structure of the response. If we interact with this response a lot, then any change to the structure of the response will mean a lot of changes to our client code. If the response is generated automatically (perhaps by calling to_json() on a hash in our Rails controller), any change to the underlying map might result in a change in the structure of the response.

Another approach would be to wrap up the response in a JavaScript class, like so:

```
ruby/groceries/spec/javascripts/userSpec.js
function User(response) {
  this.fullName = function() {
    return response.first_name + ' ' + response.last_name;
  };
}

// And in the test...
it('has a full name', function() {
  var user = new User(response);
  expect(user.fullName()).toEqual('Bob Dobilina');
});
```

Now we have the change isolation that we want though encapsulation. However, there is still one significant drawback with this approach. The functions that we're attaching to this object cannot be composed. Composability is a core strength of any functional programming language (including JavaScript), and we'd rather not give it up.

So how do we have our cake and eat it too? An approach that we've found to be effective is to create functions that operate on the response rather than attach to it. This gives us the encapsulation we want without having to wrap the response in a class, and it lets us compose the functions we create. Here's how we would handle the response:

```
ruby/groceries/public/javascripts/user.js
modit('app.user', function() {
  function fullName(user) {
    return user.first_name + ' ' + user.last_name;
  }

  function phoneBook(user) {
    return user.phone_numbers;
  }
```

```
function phoneNumbers(phoneBook) {
  return _.flatten(_.map(phoneBook, _.values));
}

this.exports(fullName, phoneNumbers, phoneBook);
});
```

This seems like an improvement over the classical approach. Now the functions are isolated from each other and can (at least in theory) be reused on other responses with the same data structure. We might have some other mailable() objects in our system, for example, and it might make sense to pull that function out into another module if we can reuse it. In any case, we can combine the few functions we've written to provide a wide array of different behavior, as we see in this example test:

ruby/groceries/spec/javascripts/userSpec.js
```
describe('a composed user', function() {
  var user;

  beforeEach(function() {
    user = require('specHelper').user;
  });

  it('has a name', function() {
    expect(user.fullName(response)).toEqual('Bob Dobilina');
  });

  it('has a phone book', function() {
    expect(user.phoneBook(response)).toContain(
      {home: '773-555-2827'},
      {mobile1: '312-555-1212'}
    );
  });

  it('makes extracting mobile phone numbers easy', function() {
    function mobile(phoneBook) {
      return _.select(phoneBook, function(entry) {
        return _.first(_.keys(entry)).indexOf('mobile') === 0;
      });
    }

    numbers = _.compose(user.phoneNumbers, mobile, user.phoneBook);

    expect(numbers(response)).toEqual(['312-555-1212', '773-555-1234']);
  });
});
```

Notice how we're combining two shared functions (phoneNumbers() and phone-Book()) with a custom function (mobile()) to create behavior that's a combination of all three. This is the power of composability.

The other major benefit we get out of this approach is testability. Instead of having to create a complete request to test our functions, we could simply create JavaScript objects that have the properties necessary to support the particular function under test. For example, instead of creating one response to rule them all in our test setup, we could have simply created individual objects with the first_name, last_name. When trying to test behavior that is highly dependent on the underlying data, this may make our tests easier to write and therefore more informative.

Gem Listing

Here is a listing of all the gems we had installed while testing the examples:

```
default.gems
abstract -v1.0.0
actionmailer -v3.0.4
actionpack -v3.0.4
activemodel -v3.0.5
activemodel -v3.0.4
activerecord -v3.0.4
activeresource -v3.0.4
activesupport -v3.0.5
activesupport -v3.0.4
addressable -v2.2.4
addressable -v2.2.3
arel -v2.0.9
arel -v2.0.8
autotest-growl -v0.2.9
bson -v1.2.0
bson_ext -v1.2.0
builder -v2.1.2
bundler -v1.0.9
diff-lcs -v1.1.2
erubis -v2.6.6
faraday -v0.5.4
faraday_middleware -v0.3.1
git -v1.2.5
haml -v3.0.25
hashie -v0.4.0
i18n -v0.5.0
jeweler -v1.5.2
mail -v2.2.15
mime-types -v1.16
mongo -v1.2.0
multi_json -v0.0.5
multi_xml -v0.2.0
multipart-post -v1.1.0
```

```
polyglot -v0.3.1
rack -v1.2.1
rack-mount -v0.6.13
rack-test -v0.5.7
rails -v3.0.4
railties -v3.0.4
rake -v0.8.7
rcov -v0.9.9
rspec -v2.5.0
rspec -v2.3.0
rspec-core -v2.5.1
rspec-core -v2.3.1
rspec-expectations -v2.5.0
rspec-expectations -v2.3.0
rspec-mocks -v2.5.0
rspec-mocks -v2.3.0
rspec-rails -v2.5.0
simple_oauth -v0.1.3
spork -v0.8.4
sqlite3 -v1.3.3
thor -v0.14.6
treetop -v1.4.9
twitter -v1.1.1
tzinfo -v0.3.24
watchr -v0.7
ZenTest -v4.4.2
```

Bibliography

[Bec02]   Kent Beck. *Test Driven Development: By Example*. Addison-Wesley, Reading, MA, 2002.

[CADH09]   David Chelimsky, Dave Astels, Zach Dennis, Aslak Hellesøy, Bryan Helmkamp, and Dan North. *The RSpec Book*. The Pragmatic Bookshelf, Raleigh, NC and Dallas, TX, 2009.

[Cro08]   Douglas Crockford. *JavaScript: The Good Parts*. O'Reilly & Associates, Inc, Sebastopol, CA, 2008.

[GHJV95]   Erich Gamma, Richard Helm, Ralph Johnson, and John Vlissides. *Design Patterns: Elements of Reusable Object-Oriented Software*. Addison-Wesley, Reading, MA, 1995.

[PP03]   Mary Poppendieck and Tom Poppendieck. *Lean Software Development: An Agile Toolkit for Software Development Managers*. Addison-Wesley, Reading, MA, 2003.

Index

Testing is only the beginning

Start with Test Driven Development, Domain Driven Design, and Acceptance Test Driven Planning in Ruby. Then add Shoulda, Cucumber, Factory Girl, and Rcov for the ultimate in Ruby and Rails development.

The RSpec Book

Behaviour-Driven Development (BDD) gives you the best of Test Driven Development, Domain Driven Design, and Acceptance Test Driven Planning techniques, so you can create better software with self-documenting, executable tests that bring users and developers together with a common language.

Get the most out of BDD in Ruby with *The RSpec Book*, written by the lead developer of RSpec, David Chelimsky.

David Chelimsky, Dave Astels, Zach Dennis, Aslak Hellesøy, Bryan Helmkamp, Dan North
(448 pages) ISBN: 9781934356371. $38.95
http://pragmaticprogrammer.com/titles/achbd

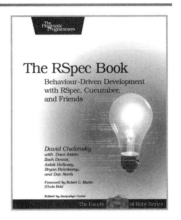

Rails Test Prescriptions

Rails Test Prescriptions is a comprehensive guide to testing Rails applications, covering Test-Driven Development from both a theoretical perspective (why to test) and from a practical perspective (how to test effectively). It covers the core Rails testing tools and procedures for Rails 2 and Rails 3, and introduces popular add-ons, including RSpec, Shoulda, Cucumber, Factory Girl, and Rcov.

Noel Rappin
(368 pages) ISBN: 9781934356647. $34.95
http://pragmaticprogrammer.com/titles/nrtest

Welcome to the New Web

The world isn't quite ready for the new web standards, but you can be. Get started with HTML5, CSS3, and a better JavaScript today.

CoffeeScript

CoffeeScript is JavaScript done right. It provides all of JavaScript's functionality wrapped in a cleaner, more succinct syntax. In the first book on this exciting new language, CoffeeScript guru Trevor Burnham shows you how to hold onto all the power and flexibility of JavaScript while writing clearer, cleaner, and safer code.

Trevor Burnham
(136 pages) ISBN: 9781934356784. $29
http://pragmaticprogrammer.com/titles/tbcoffee

HTML5 and CSS3

HTML5 and CSS3 are the future of web development, but you don't have to wait to start using them. Even though the specification is still in development, many modern browsers and mobile devices already support HTML5 and CSS3. This book gets you up to speed on the new HTML5 elements and CSS3 features you can use right now, and backwards compatible solutions ensure that you don't leave users of older browsers behind.

Brian P. Hogan
(280 pages) ISBN: 9781934356685. $33
http://pragmaticprogrammer.com/titles/bhh5

Be Agile

Don't just "do" agile; you want *be* agile. We'll show you how.

Agile in a Flash

The best agile book isn't a book: *Agile in a Flash* is a unique deck of index cards that fit neatly in your pocket. You can tape them to the wall. Spread them out on your project table. Get stains on them over lunch. These cards are meant to be used, not just read.

Jeff Langr and Tim Ottinger
(110 pages) ISBN: 9781934356715. $15
http://pragmaticprogrammer.com/titles/olag

The Agile Samurai

Here are three simple truths about software development:

1. You can't gather all the requirements up front. 2. The requirements you do gather will change. 3. There is always more to do than time and money will allow.

Those are the facts of life. But you can deal with those facts (and more) by becoming a fierce software-delivery professional, capable of dispatching the most dire of software projects and the toughest delivery schedules with ease and grace.

Jonathan Rasmusson
(280 pages) ISBN: 9781934356586. $34.95
http://pragmaticprogrammer.com/titles/jtrap

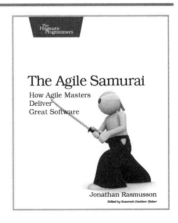

Advanced Ruby and Rails

What used to be the realm of experts is fast becoming the stuff of day-to-day development. Jump to the head of the class in Ruby and Rails.

Crafting Rails Applications

Rails 3 is a huge step forward. You can now easily extend the framework, change its behavior, and replace whole components to bend it to your will, all without messy hacks. This pioneering book is the first resource that deep dives into the new Rails 3 APIs and shows you how to use them to write better web applications and make your day-to-day work with Rails more productive.

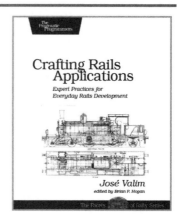

José Valim
(180 pages) ISBN: 9781934356739. $33
http://pragmaticprogrammer.com/titles/jvrails

Metaprogramming Ruby

As a Ruby programmer, you already know how much fun it is. Now see how to unleash its power, digging under the surface and exploring the language's most advanced features: a collection of techniques and tricks known as *metaprogramming*. Once the domain of expert Rubyists, metaprogramming is now accessible to programmers of all levels—from beginner to expert. *Metaprogramming Ruby* explains metaprogramming concepts in a down-to-earth style and arms you with a practical toolbox that will help you write great Ruby code.

Paolo Perrotta
(240 pages) ISBN: 9781934356470. $32.95
http://pragmaticprogrammer.com/titles/ppmetr

Ruby on the JVM and More Languages

Want to integrate Ruby within your Enterprise JVM environment? JRuby is the answer. And when you're ready to expand your horizons, we've got seven major languages worthy of your study.

Using JRuby

Now you can bring the best of Ruby into the world of Java, with *Using JRuby*. Come to the source for the JRuby core team's insights and insider tips. You'll learn how to call Java objects seamlessly from Ruby, and deal with Java idioms such as interfaces and overloaded functions. Run Ruby code from Java, and make a Java program scriptable in Ruby. See how to compile Ruby into .class files that are callable from Java, Scala, Clojure, or any other JVM language.

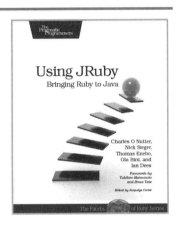

Charles O Nutter, Thomas Enebo, Nick Sieger, Ola Bini, and Ian Dees
(300 pages) ISBN: 9781934356654. $34.95
http://pragmaticprogrammer.com/titles/jruby

Seven Languages in Seven Weeks

You should learn a programming language every year, as recommended by *The Pragmatic Programmer*. But if one per year is good, how about *Seven Languages in Seven Weeks*? In this book you'll get a hands-on tour of Clojure, Haskell, Io, Prolog, Scala, Erlang, and Ruby. Whether or not your favorite language is on that list, you'll broaden your perspective of programming by examining these languages side-by-side. You'll learn something new from each, and best of all, you'll learn how to learn a language quickly.

Bruce A. Tate
(300 pages) ISBN: 9781934356593. $34.95
http://pragmaticprogrammer.com/titles/btlang

Pragmatic Guide Series

If you want to know what lies ahead, ask those who are coming back. Our pragmatic authors have been there, they've done it, and they've come back to help guide you along the road. They'll get you started quickly, with a minimum of fuss and hand-holding. The Pragmatic Guide Series features convenient, task-oriented two-page spreads. You'll find what you need fast, and get on with your work

Pragmatic Guide to Git

Need to learn how to wrap your head around Git, but don't need a lot of hand holding? Grab this book if you're new to Git, not to the world of programming. Git tasks displayed on two-page spreads provide all the context you need, without the extra fluff.

NEW: Part of the new *Pragmatic Guide* series

Travis Swicegood
(168 pages) ISBN: 9781934356722. $25
http://pragmaticprogrammer.com/titles/pg_git

Pragmatic Guide to JavaScript

JavaScript is everywhere. It's a key component of to-day's Web—a powerful, dynamic language with a rich ecosystem of professional-grade development tools, infrastructures, frameworks, and toolkits. This book will get you up to speed quickly and painlessly with the 35 key JavaScript tasks you need to know.

NEW: Part of the new *Pragmatic Guide* series

Christophe Porteneuve
(150 pages) ISBN: 9781934356678. $25
http://pragmaticprogrammer.com/titles/pg_js

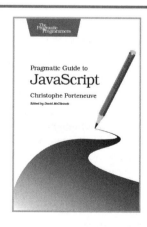

Pragmatic Practices

Pragmatic Programmers *think* about their practices and improve them. Start here.

Pragmatic Thinking and Learning

Software development happens in your head. Not in an editor, IDE, or design tool. You're well educated on how to work with software and hardware, but what about *wetware*—our own brains? Learning new skills and new technology is critical to your career, and it's all in your head.

In this book by Andy Hunt, you'll learn how our brains are wired, and how to take advantage of your brain's architecture. You'll learn new tricks and tips to learn more, faster, and retain more of what you learn.

You need a pragmatic approach to thinking and learning. You need to *Refactor Your Wetware*.

Andy Hunt
(288 pages) ISBN: 9781934356050. $34.95
http://pragmaticprogrammer.com/titles/ahptl

Pomodoro Technique Illustrated

Do you ever look at the clock and wonder where the day went? You spent all this time at work and didn't come close to getting everything done. Tomorrow, try something new. Use the Pomodoro Technique, originally developed by Francesco Cirillo, to work in focused sprints throughout the day. In *Pomodoro Technique Illustrated*, Staffan Nöteberg shows you how to organize your work to accomplish more in less time. There's no need for expensive software or fancy planners. You can get started with nothing more than a piece of paper, a pencil, and a kitchen timer.

Staffan Nöteberg
(144 pages) ISBN: 9781934356500. $24.95
http://pragmaticprogrammer.com/titles/snfocus

The Pragmatic Bookshelf

The Pragmatic Bookshelf features books written by developers for developers. The titles continue the well-known Pragmatic Programmer style and continue to garner awards and rave reviews. As development gets more and more difficult, the Pragmatic Programmers will be there with more titles and products to help you stay on top of your game.

Visit Us Online

This Book's Home Page
http://pragprog.com/titles/rcctr
Source code from this book, errata, and other resources. Come give us feedback, too!

Register for Updates
http://pragprog.com/updates
Be notified when updates and new books become available.

Join the Community
http://pragprog.com/community
Read our weblogs, join our online discussions, participate in our mailing list, interact with our wiki, and benefit from the experience of other Pragmatic Programmers.

New and Noteworthy
http://pragprog.com/news
Check out the latest pragmatic developments, new titles and other offerings.

Save on the eBook

Save on the eBook versions of this title. Owning the paper version of this book entitles you to purchase the electronic versions at a terrific discount.

PDFs are great for carrying around on your laptop—they are hyperlinked, have color, and are fully searchable. Most titles are also available for the iPhone and iPod touch, Amazon Kindle, and other popular e-book readers.

Buy now at *http://pragprog.com/coupon*

Contact Us

Online Orders:	*http://pragprog.com/catalog*
Customer Service:	*support@pragprog.com*
International Rights:	*translations@pragprog.com*
Academic Use:	*academic@pragprog.com*
Write for Us:	*http://pragprog.com/write-for-use*
Or Call:	+1 800-699-7764